EASY PIANO

Christmas Romance

CONTENTS

ISBN 0-634-04757-4

HAL•LEONARD®
CORPORATION
7777 W. BLUEMOUND RD. P.O. BOX 13819 MILWAUKEE, WI 53213

Visit Hal Leonard Online at
www.halleonard.com

ALL I WANT FOR CHRISTMAS IS YOU

Words and Music by MARIAH CAREY
and WALTER AFANASIEFF

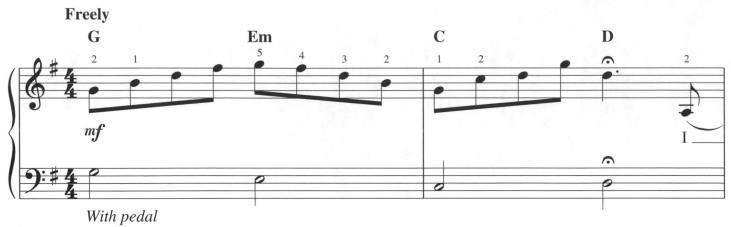

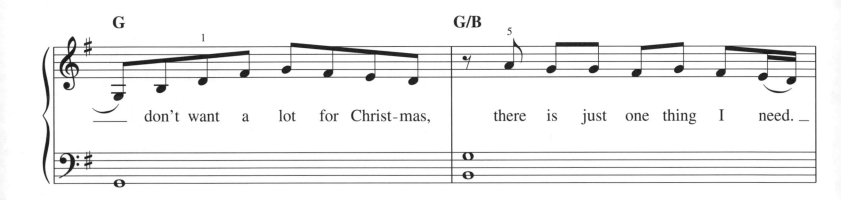

don't want a lot for Christ-mas, there is just one thing I need. __

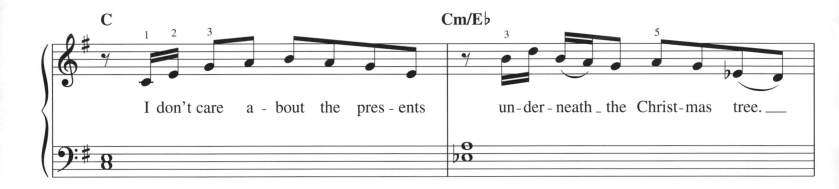

I don't care a - bout the pres - ents un - der - neath __ the Christ-mas tree. __

I just want you for my own, more than you could ev - er know.

Make my wish come true: ___ all I ___ want for Christ-mas is you. ___

Moderately

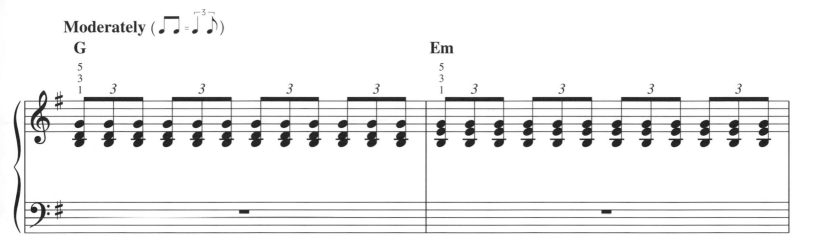

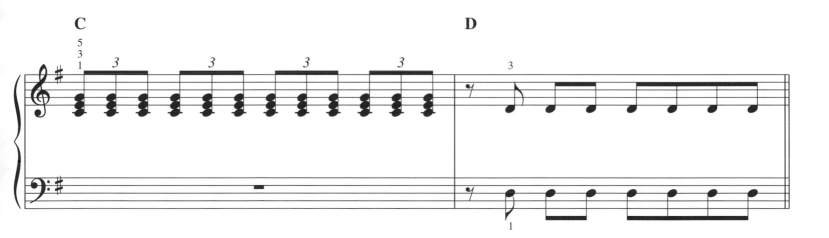

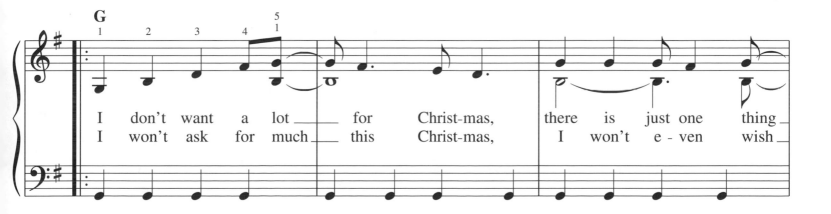

I don't want a lot ___ for Christ-mas, there is just one thing
I won't ask for much ___ this Christ-mas, I won't e - ven wish

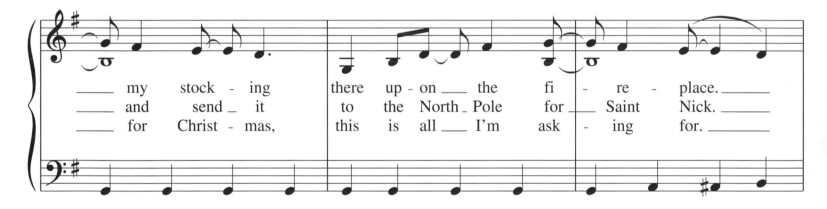

- mas day. ___ / I just want you for ___ my own, ___
- deer click. ___ / I just want you here ___ to - night, ___
___ my door. ___ / I just want him for ___ my own;

G   B7

Em   Cm6/E♭   G/D

more than you could ev - er know. ___ / Make my wish come true:
hold - ing on to me ___ so tight. ___ / What more can I do?
more than you could ev - er know. ___ / Make my wish come true:___

To Coda

E7   Am9   Am7♭5/D

Ba - by, all I want for Christ - mas is

G   Em

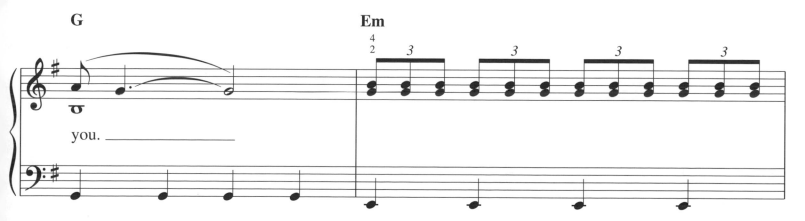

you. ___

You, _____ ba - by. __ Oh, _____ ba - by. __ Oh,

__ all the lights __ are shin - ing so bright - ly ev - 'ry - where,

_____ and the sound __ of chil - dren's

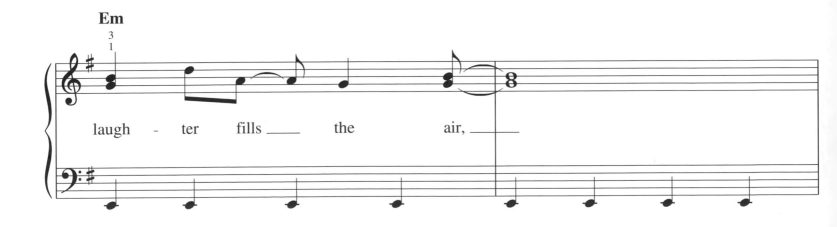

laugh - ter fills __ the air, ____

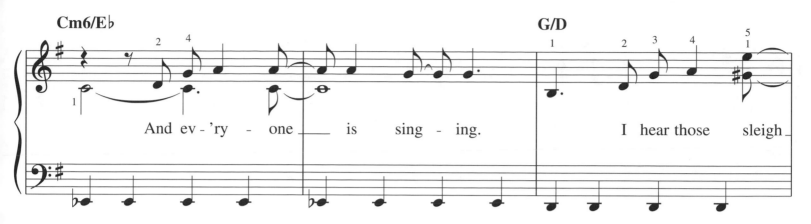

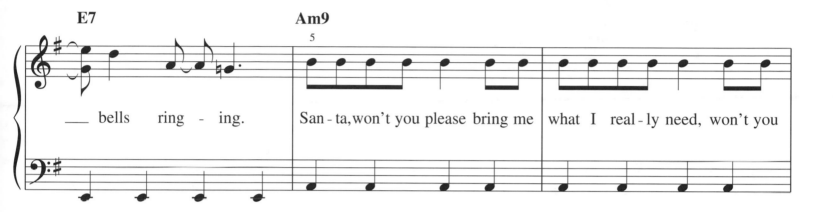

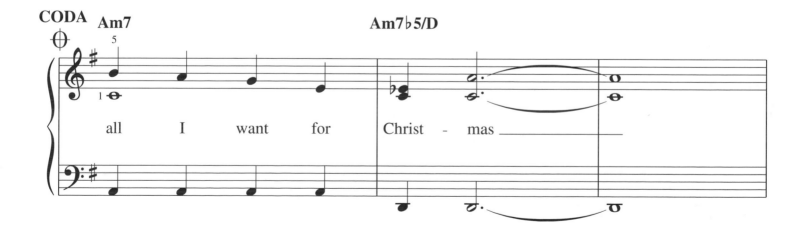

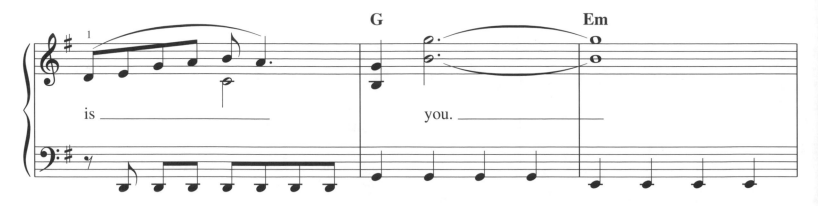

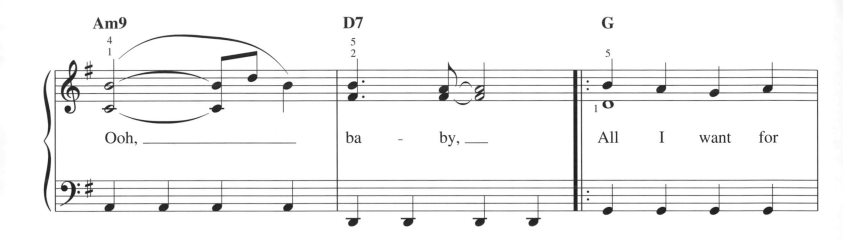

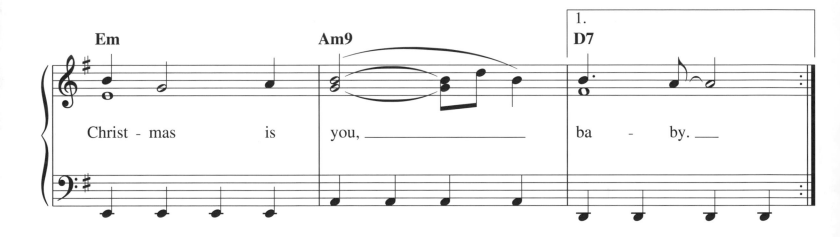

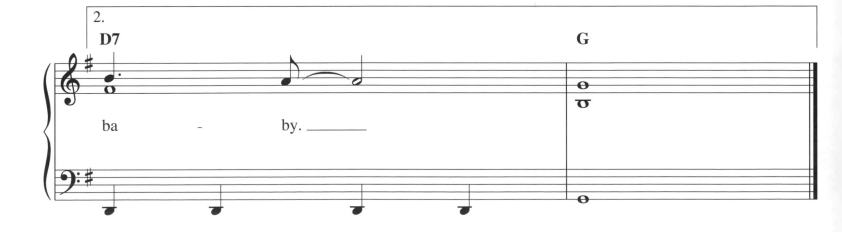

AS LONG AS THERE'S CHRISTMAS

from Walt Disney's BEAUTY AND THE BEAST - THE ENCHANTED CHRISTMAS

Music by RACHEL PORTMAN
Lyrics by DON BLACK

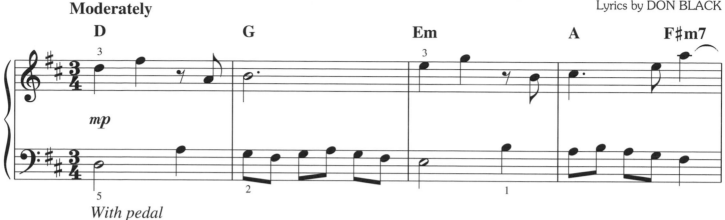

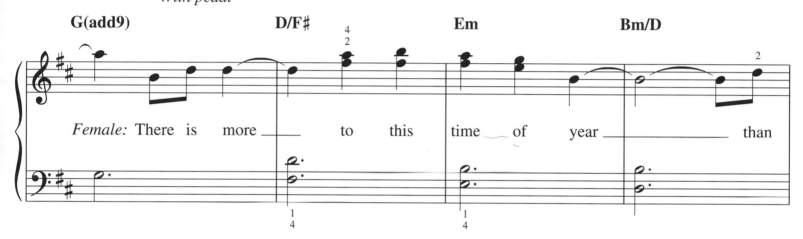

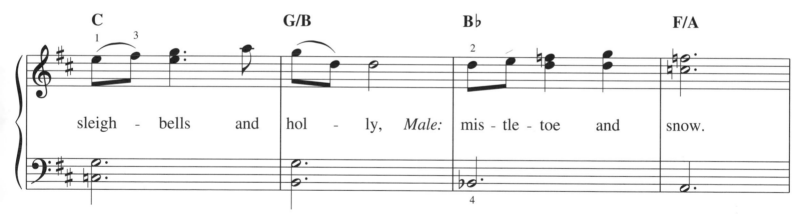

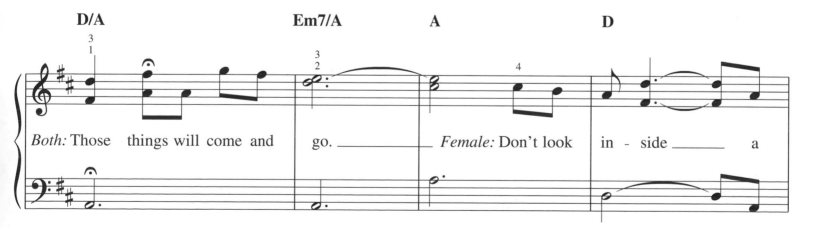

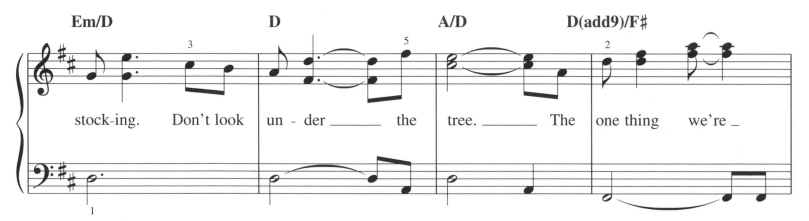

stock-ing. Don't look | un - der _____ the | tree. _____ The | one thing we're _

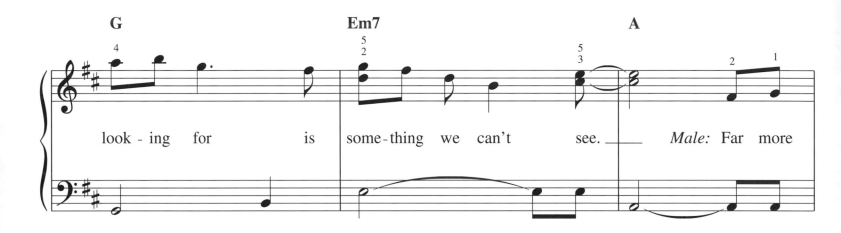

look - ing for | is | some-thing we can't | see. _____ *Male:* Far more

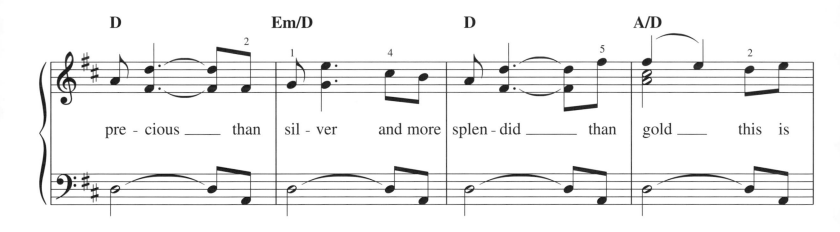

pre - cious _____ than | sil - ver | and more splen-did _____ than | gold ____ this is

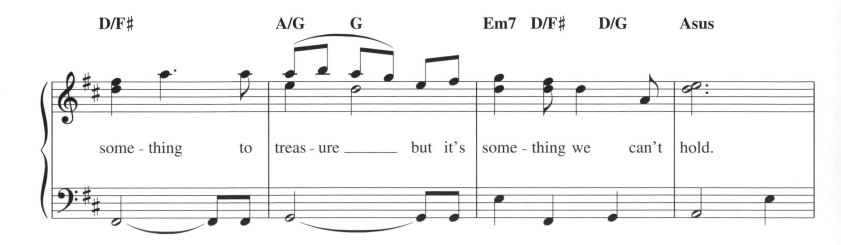

some - thing to | treas - ure _____ but it's | some - thing we can't | hold.

Oh, __ *Both:* As long as there's Christ-mas, I tru-ly be-

lieve *Male:* that hope is the great-est *Both:* of the

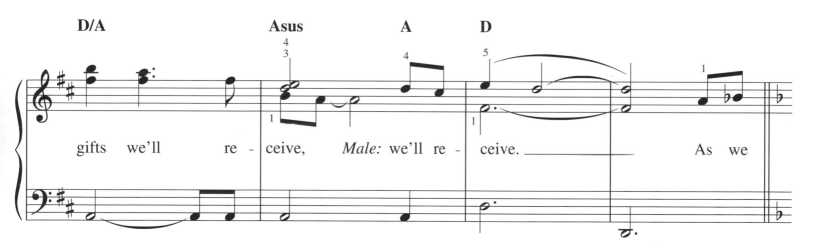

gifts we'll re-ceive, *Male:* we'll re-ceive. ___ As we

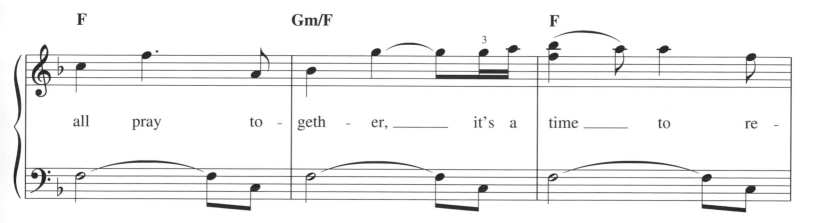

all pray to-geth-er, ___ it's a time ___ to re-

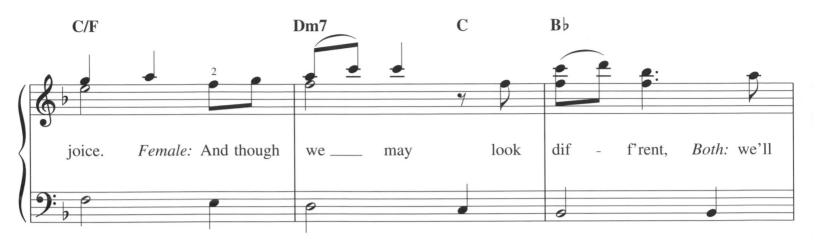

joice. *Female:* And though we ____ may look dif - f'rent, *Both:* we'll

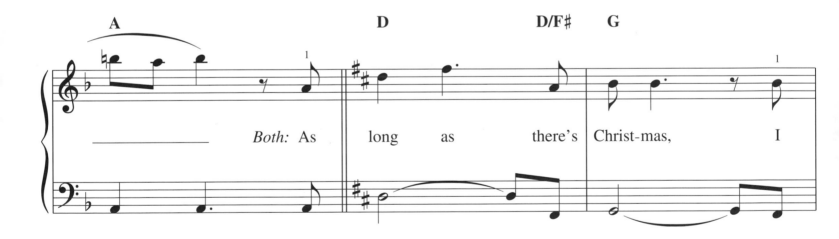

all sing with one voice. ____ *Male:* Whoa. ____

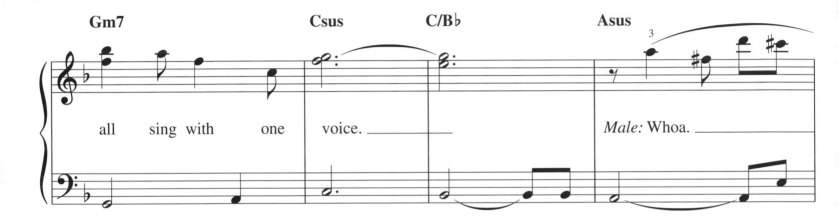

____ *Both:* As long as there's Christ-mas, I

tru - ly be - lieve that hope is the great-est of the

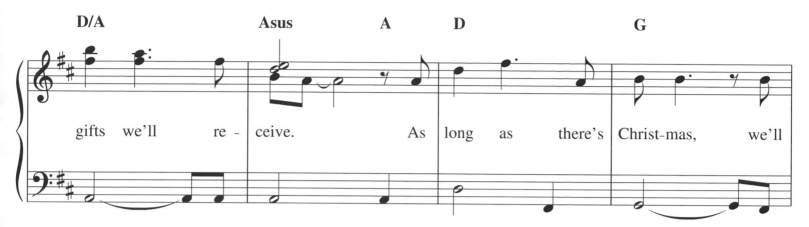

gifts we'll re - ceive. As long as there's Christ-mas, we'll

all be just fine. A star shines a - bove us, _____ light-ing

Female:

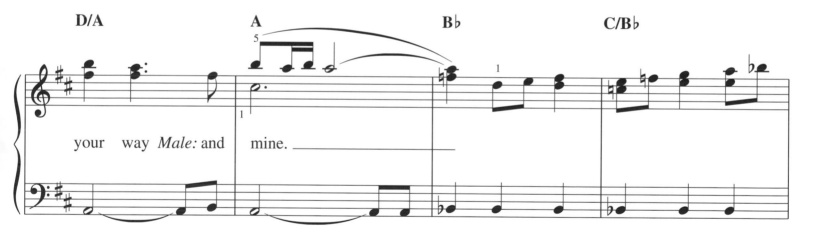

your way *Male:* and mine. _____

Female: Oh. _____ *Male:* Light my way.

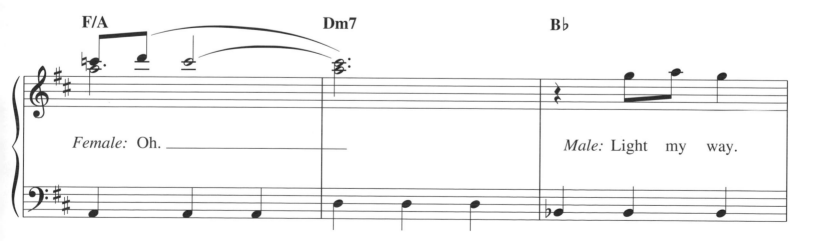

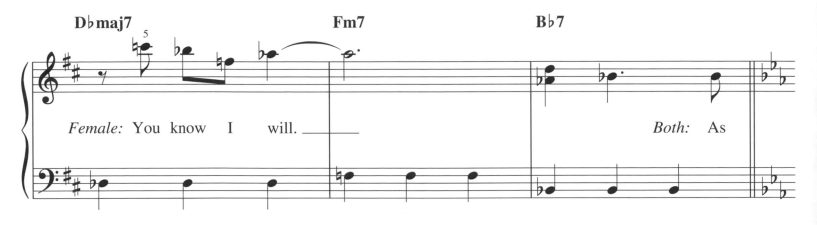

Db maj7　　　　**Fm7**　　　　**Bb7**

Female: You know I will. ＿＿＿　　　　*Both:* As

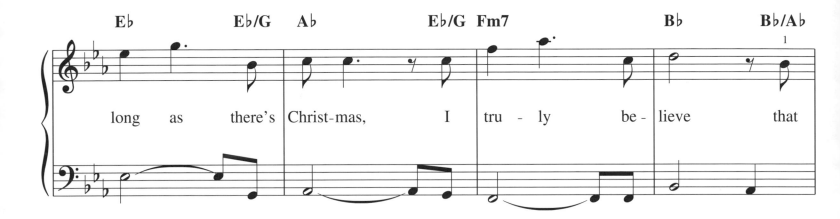

Eb　　**Eb/G**　**Ab**　　　**Eb/G**　**Fm7**　　　　**Bb**　　**Bb/Ab**

long as there's Christ-mas, I tru - ly be - lieve that

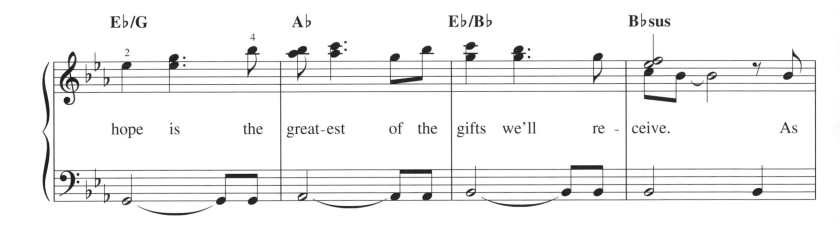

Eb/G　　　　**Ab**　　　　**Eb/Bb**　　　　**Bb sus**

hope is the great-est of the gifts we'll re - ceive. As

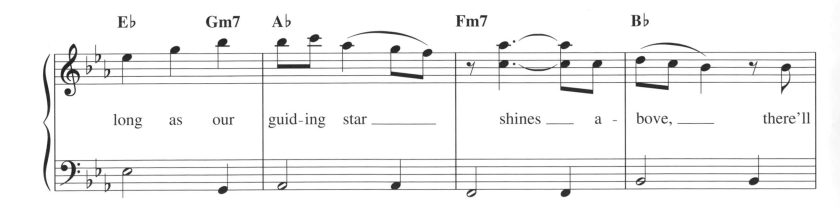

Eb　　**Gm7**　**Ab**　　　　**Fm7**　　　　**Bb**

long as our guid-ing star ＿＿＿ shines ＿ a - bove, ＿＿＿ there'll

al - ways be Christ - mas _____ *Male:* so there al - ways will

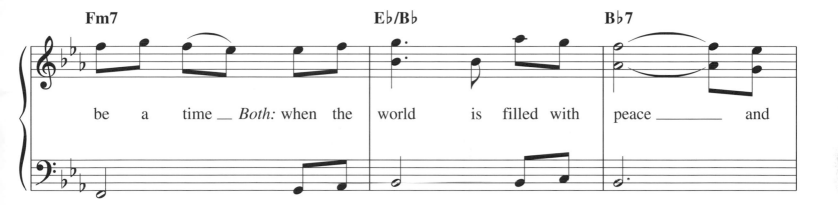

be a time _ *Both:* when the world is filled with peace _____ and

love. __

Because It's Christmas

(For All the Children)

Music by BARRY MANILOW
Lyric by BRUCE SUSSMAN and JACK FELDMAN

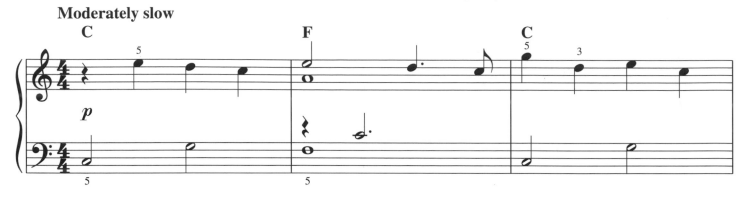

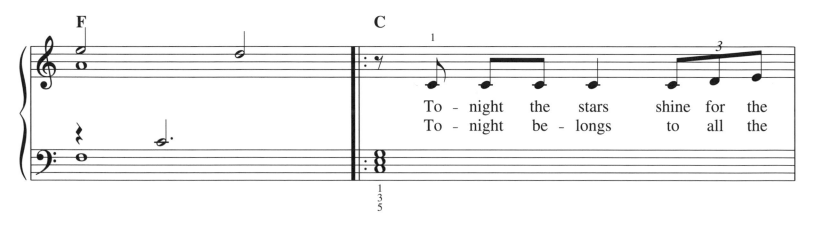

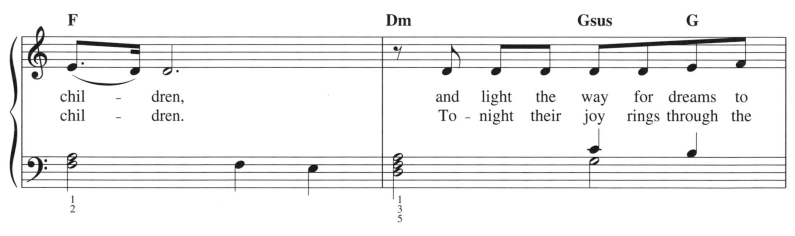

rib - bons.
bless - ings

The world is right and hopes are
to all the chil - dren ev - 'ry -

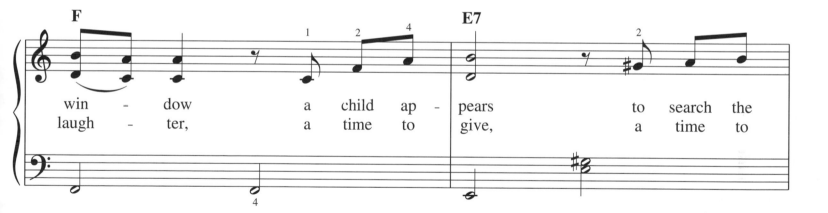

high.
where,

And from a dark and frost - ed
to see the smiles and hear the

win - dow a child ap - pears to search the
laugh - ter, a time to give, a time to

sky be-cause it's Christ - mas, be-cause it's Christ - mas.
share be-cause it's

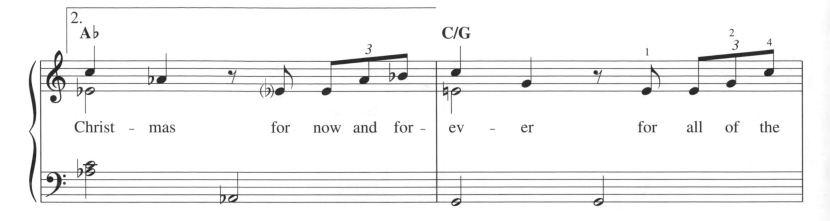

Christ – mas   for   now and for – ev – er   for   all of the

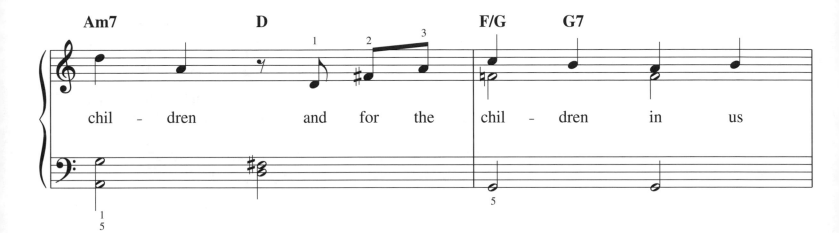

chil – dren   and   for   the   chil – dren   in   us

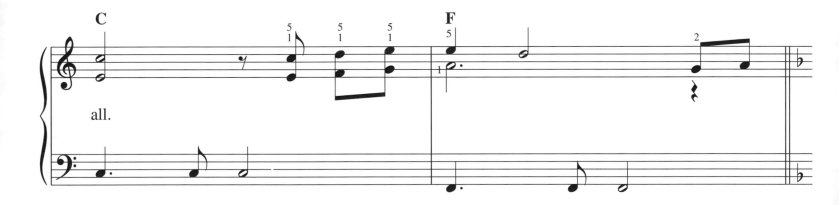

all.

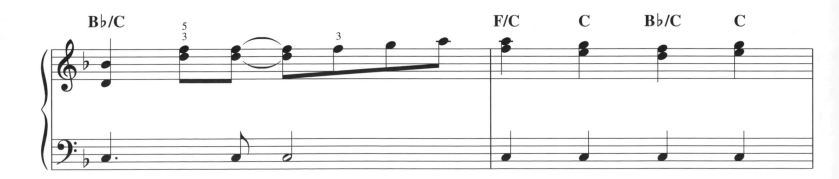

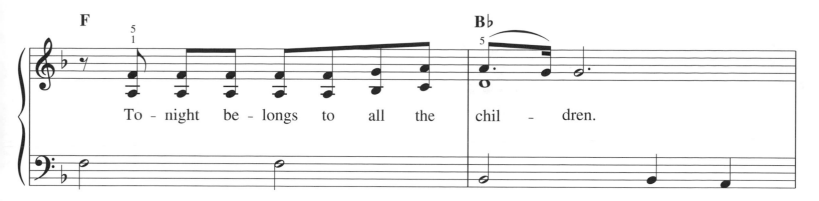

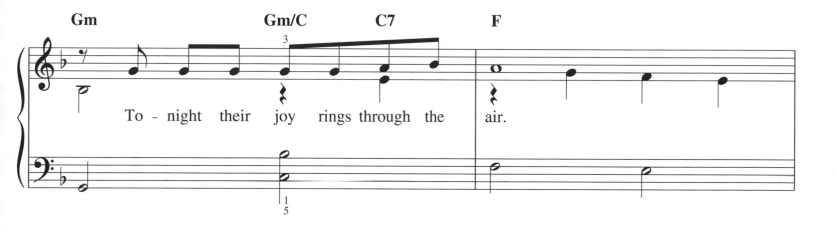

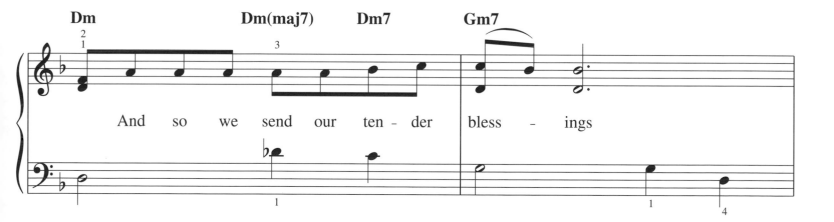

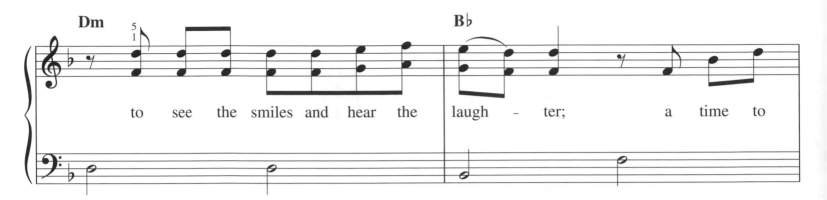

to see the smiles and hear the laugh - ter; a time to

give, a time to share be-cause it's Christ - mas for now and for-

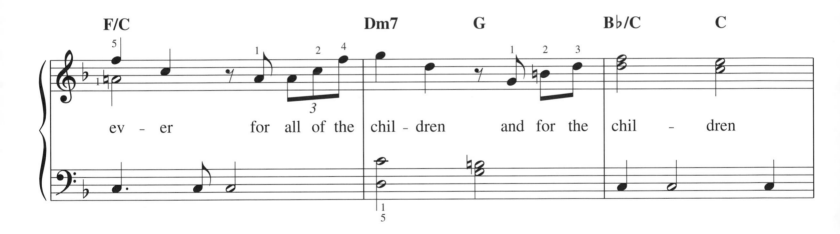

ev - er for all of the chil - dren and for the chil - dren

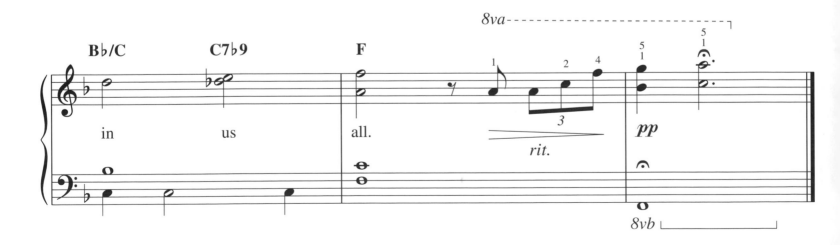

in us all. *pp*

rit.

THE CHRISTMAS SONG
(Chestnuts Roasting on an Open Fire)

Music and Lyric by MEL TORME
and ROBERT WELLS

Chest-nuts roast-ing on an o-pen fire, Jack Frost nip-ping at your

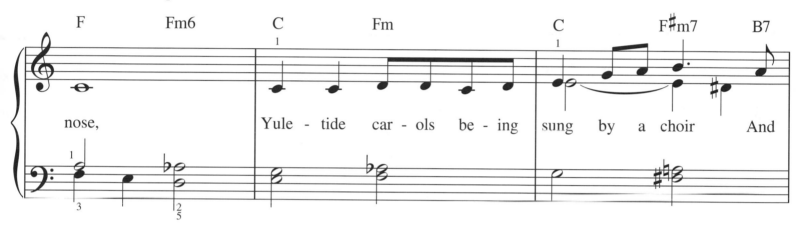

nose, Yule-tide car-ols be-ing sung by a choir And

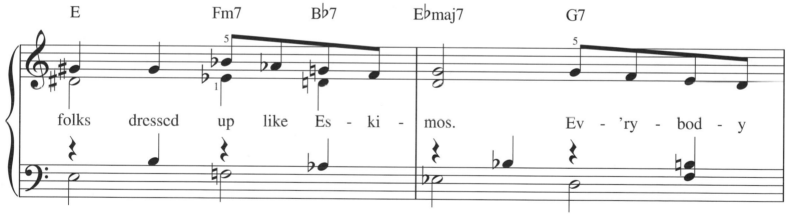

folks dressed up like Es-ki-mos. Ev-'ry-bod-y

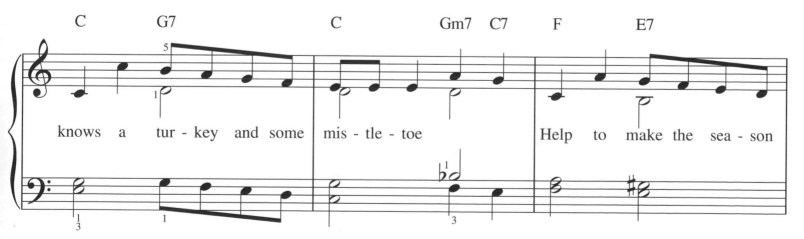

knows a tur-key and some mis-tle-toe Help to make the sea-son

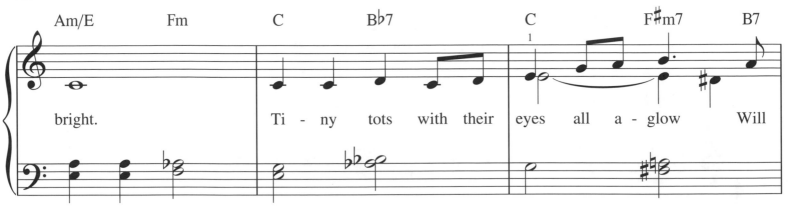

bright. Ti - ny tots with their eyes all a - glow Will

find it hard to sleep to - night. They know that San - ta's on his

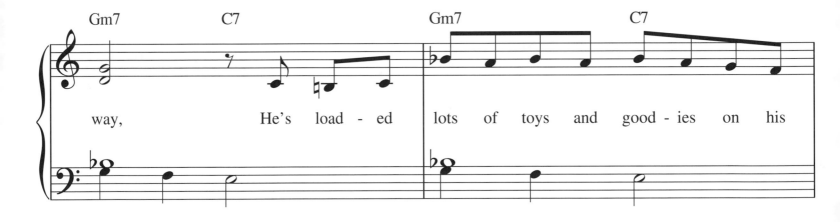

way, He's load - ed lots of toys and good - ies on his

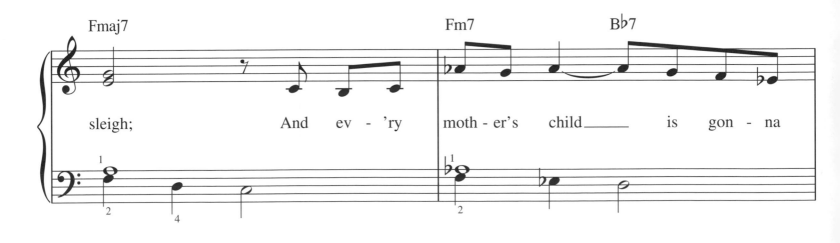

sleigh; And ev - 'ry moth - er's child_____ is gon - na

Ebmaj7   Am7   Ab7

spy _____ To see if rein - deer real - ly know how to

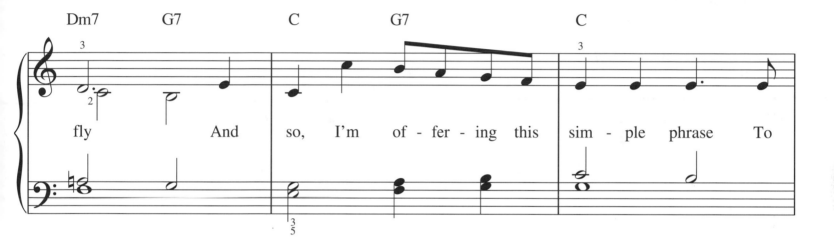

Dm7   G7   C   G7   C

fly   And so, I'm of - fer - ing this sim - ple phrase To

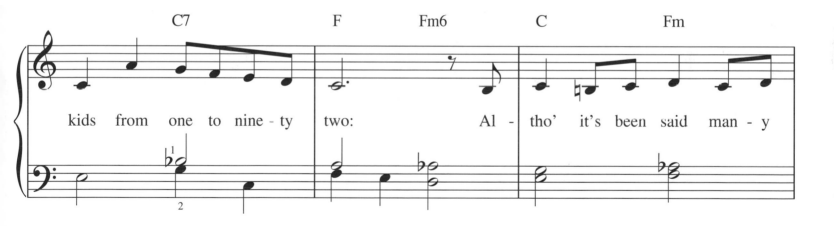

C7   F   Fm6   C   Fm

kids from one to nine - ty two: Al - tho' it's been said man - y

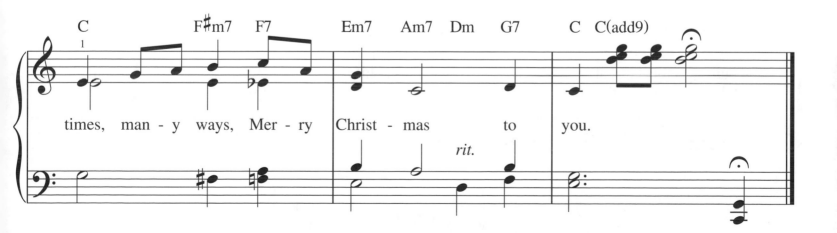

C   F#m7   F7   Em7   Am7   Dm   G7   C   C(add9)

times, man - y ways, Mer - ry Christ - mas to you.

rit.

CHRISTMAS TIME IS HERE

from A CHARLIE BROWN CHRISTMAS

Words by LEE MENDELSON
Music by VINCE GUARALDI

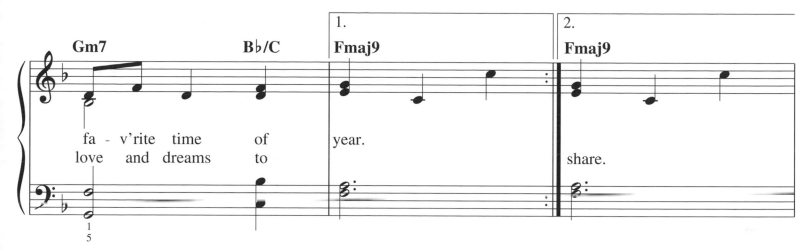

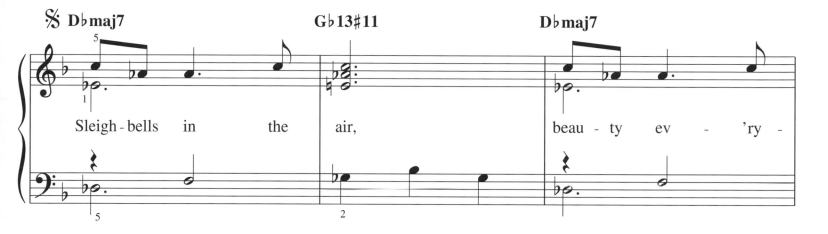

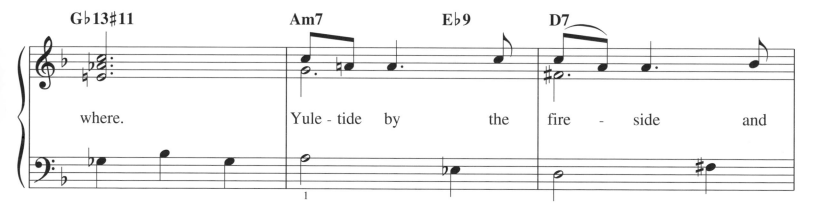

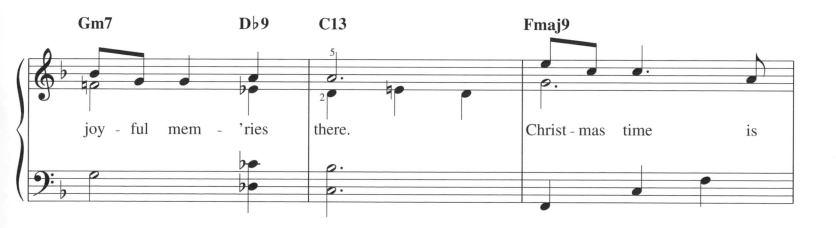

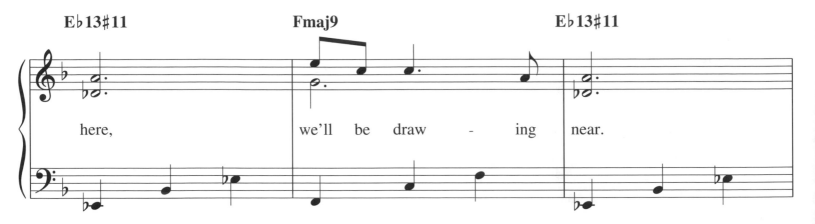

To Coda ⊕

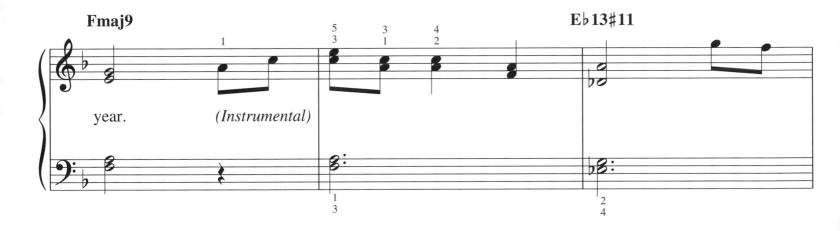

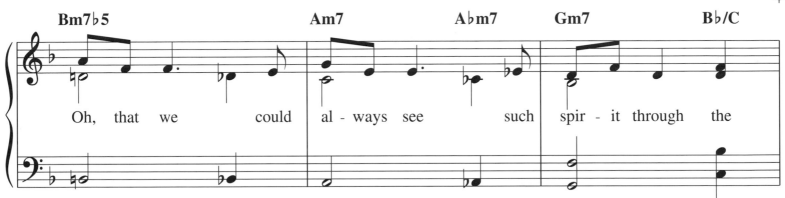

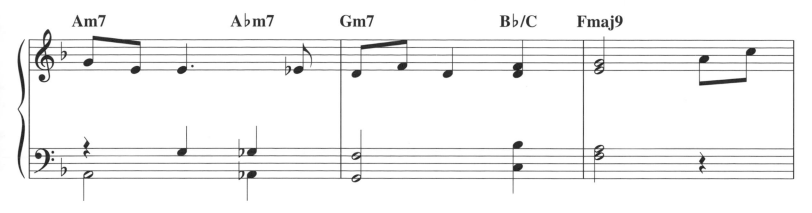

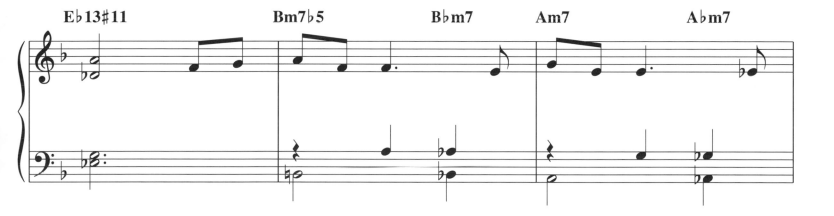

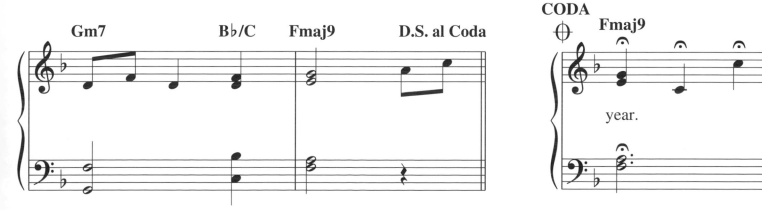

THE CHRISTMAS WALTZ

Words by SAMMY CAHN
Music by JULE STYNE

Moderately slow, with expression

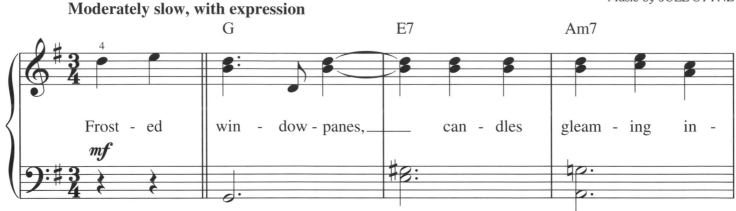

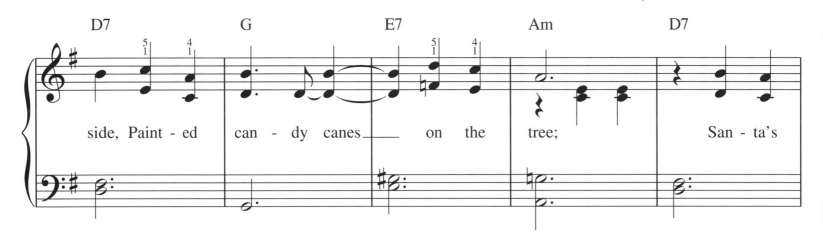

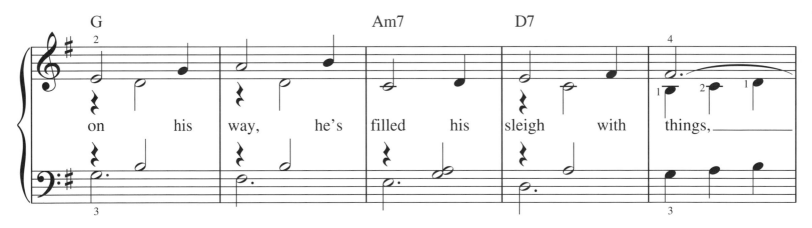

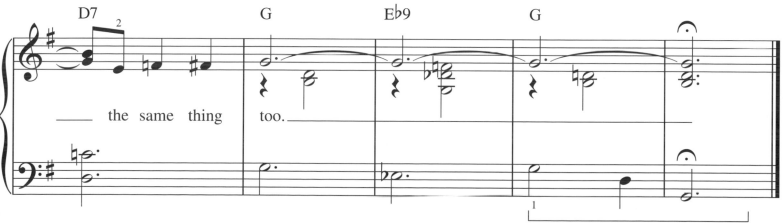

THE GIFT

Words and Music by TOM DOUGLAS
and JIM BRICKMAN

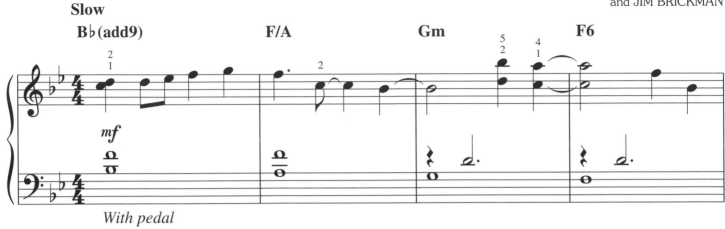

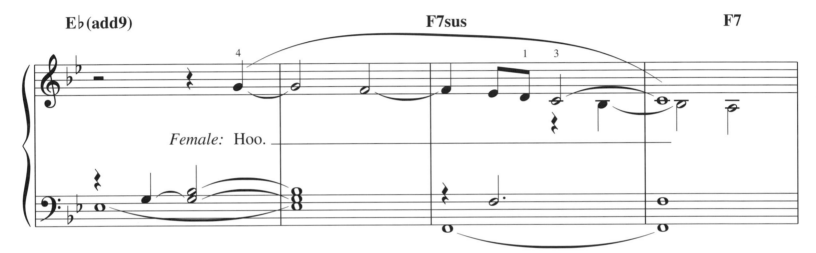

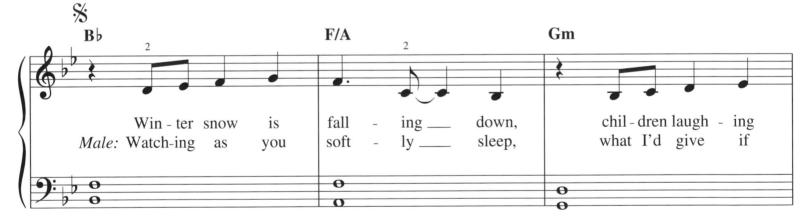

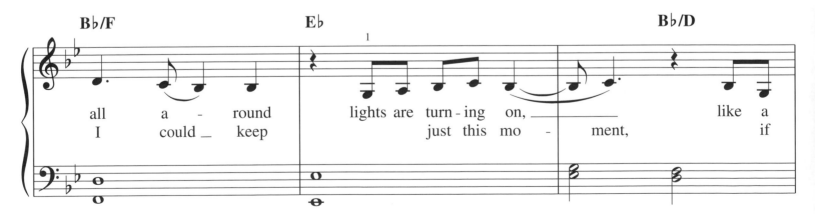

Cm7 · Fsus · F · Bb

fair - y tale __ come true. __
on - ly time __ stood still. __

Sit - ting by the fire __
But the col - ors fade __

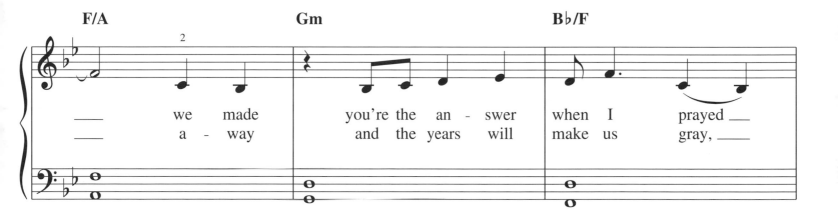

F/A · Gm · Bb/F

__ we made
__ a - way

you're the an - swer
and the years will

when I prayed __
make us gray, __

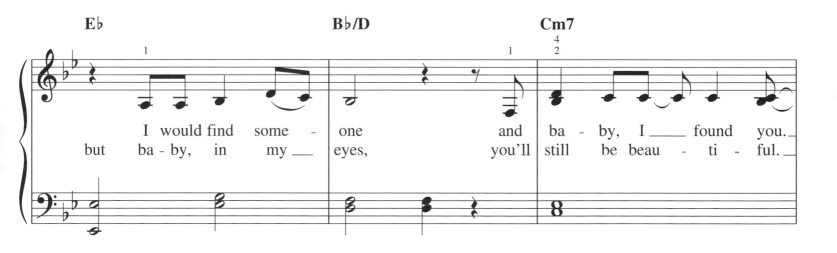

Eb · Bb/D · Cm7

I would find some - one
but ba - by, in my __ eyes,

and ba - by, I __ found you. __
you'll still be beau - ti - ful. __

F7sus · F · Bb/D

Both: All I want __ is to hold __

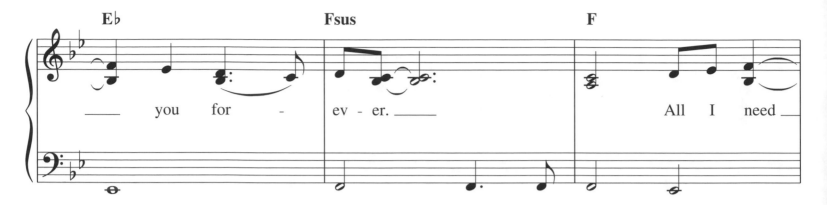

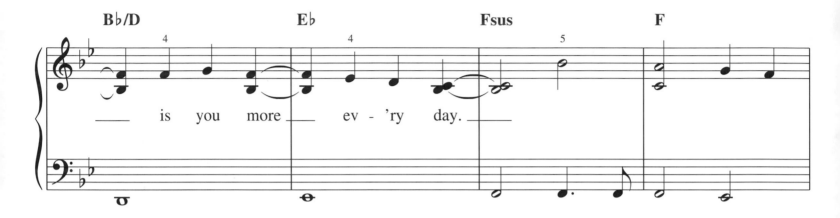

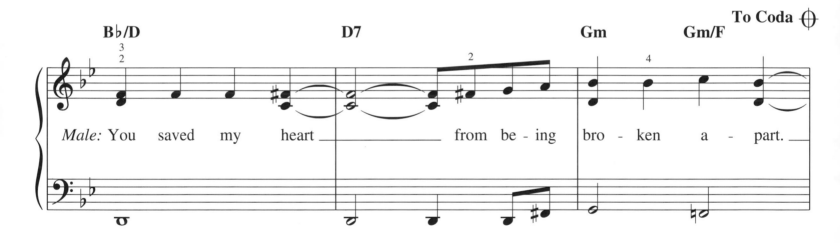

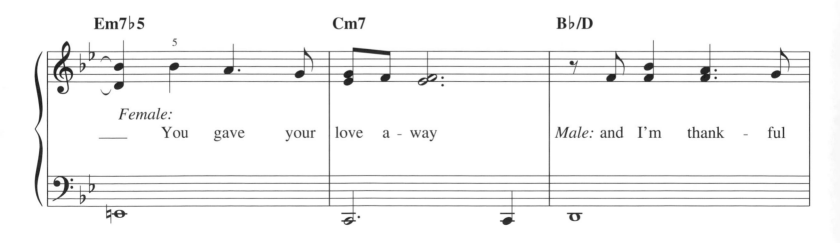

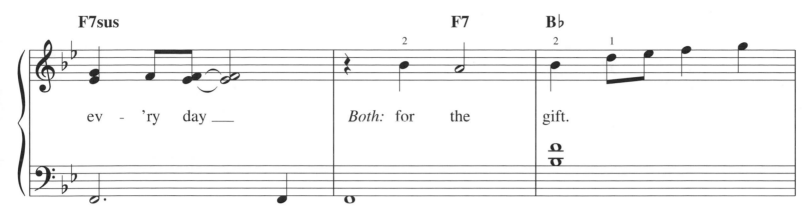

ev - 'ry day ___ *Both:* for the gift.

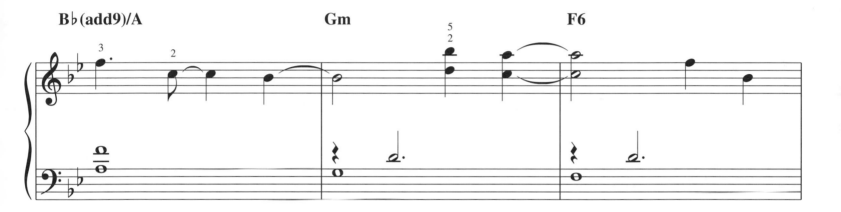

D.S. al Coda

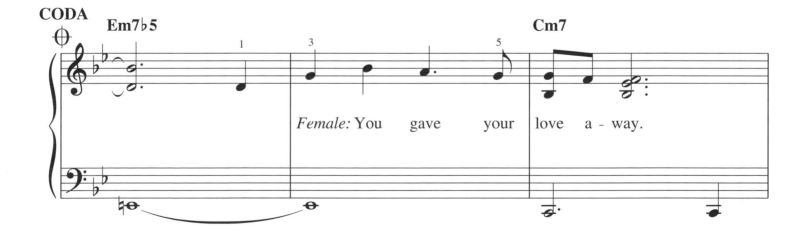

Female: You gave your love a - way.

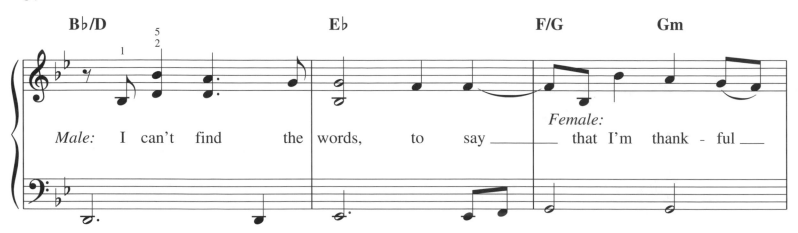

Male: I can't find the words, to say _____ that I'm thank - ful _____

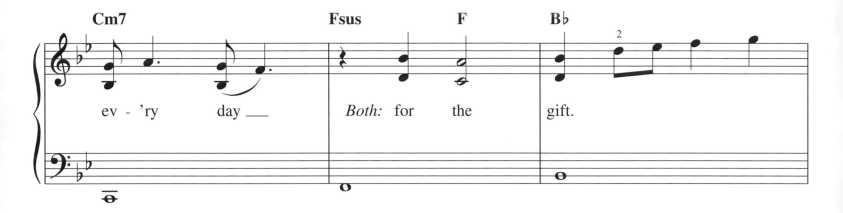

ev - 'ry day ___ Both: for the gift.

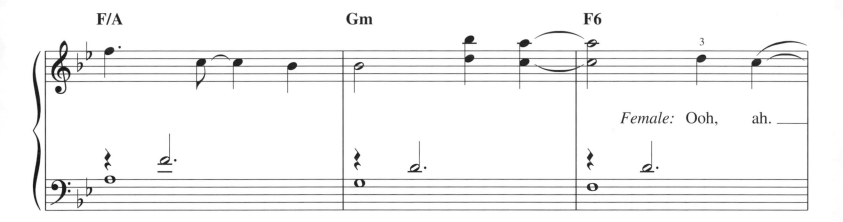

Female: Ooh, ah.

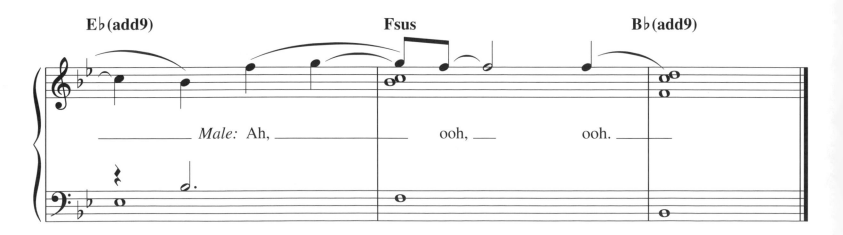

_____ Male: Ah, _____ ooh, ___ ooh. _____

(There's No Place Like)
HOME FOR THE HOLIDAYS

Words by AL STILLMAN
Music by ROBERT ALLEN

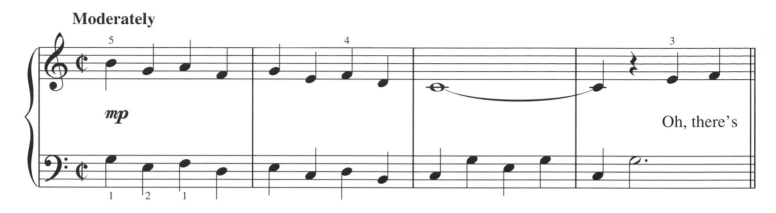

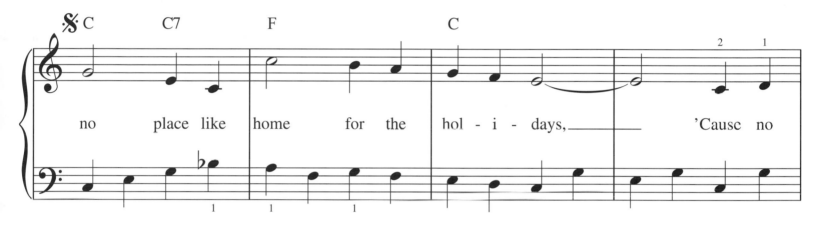

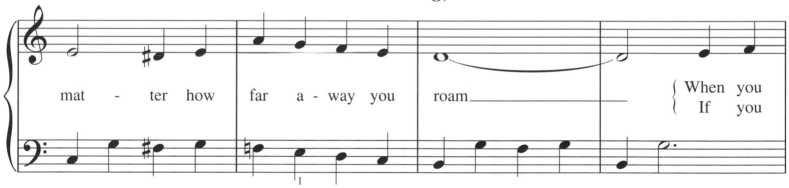

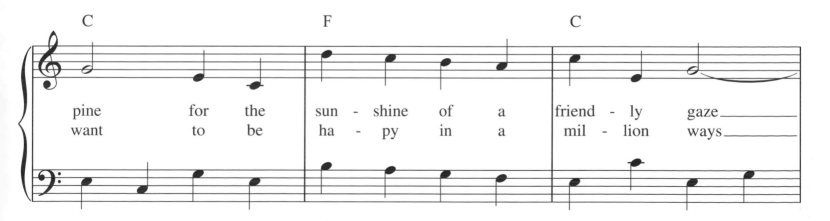

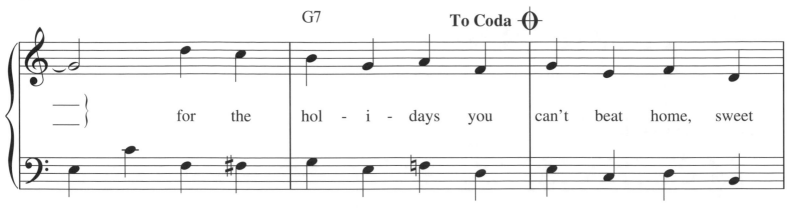

for the hol - i - days you can't beat home, sweet

home. I met a man who lives in

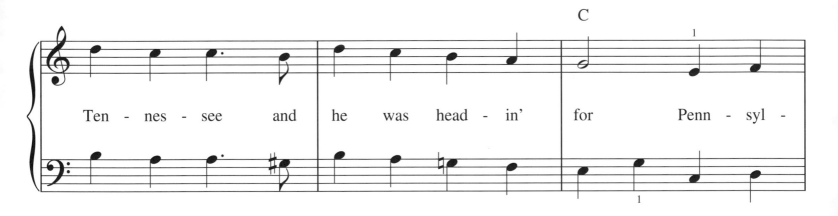

Ten - nes - see and he was head - in' for Penn - syl -

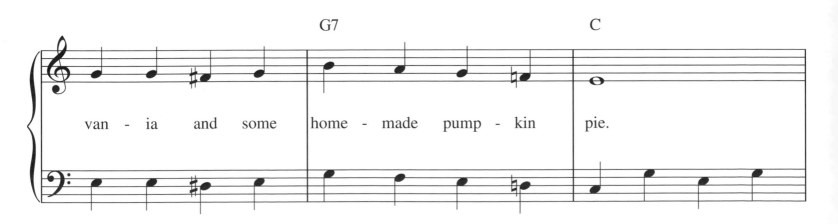

van - ia and some home - made pump - kin pie.

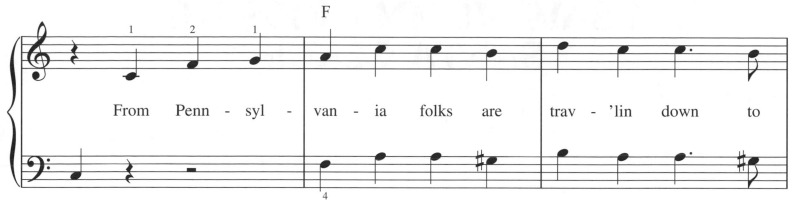

From Penn - syl - van - ia folks are trav - 'lin down to

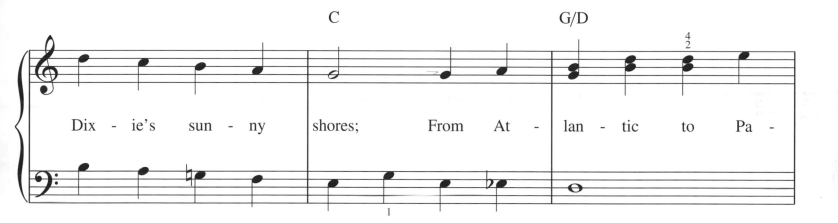

Dix - ie's sun - ny shores; From At - lan - tic to Pa -

cif - ic, gee, the traf - fic is ter - rif - ic. Oh, there's

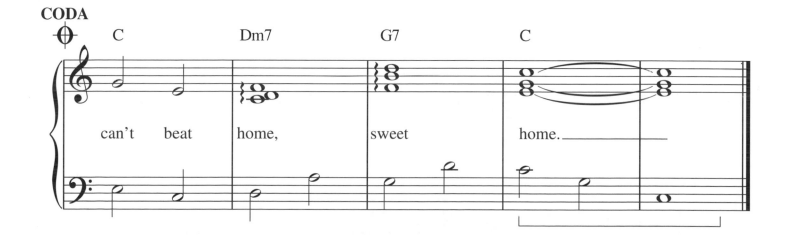

can't beat home, sweet home.___

I SAW MOMMY KISSING SANTA CLAUS

Words and Music by
TOMMIE CONNOR

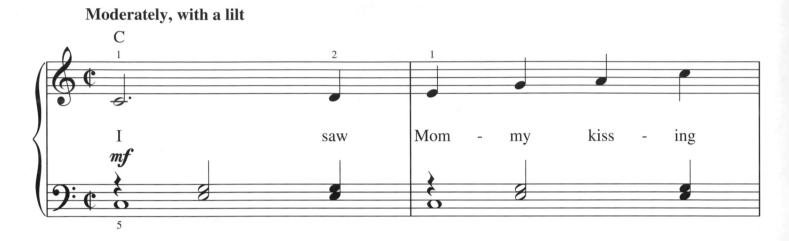

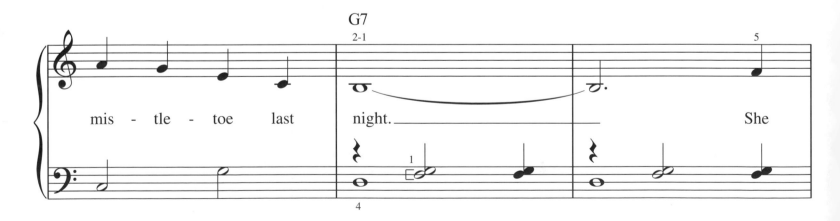

did - n't see me creep down the stairs to have a

peep; She thought that I was tucked up in my

bed - room fast a - sleep. Then I saw

Mom - my tick - le San - ta Claus

un - der - neath his beard so snow - y white. ____

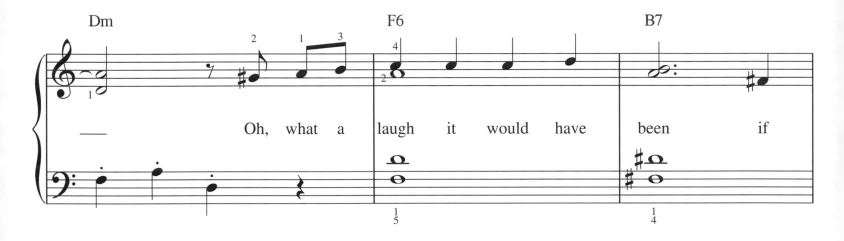

____ Oh, what a laugh it would have been if

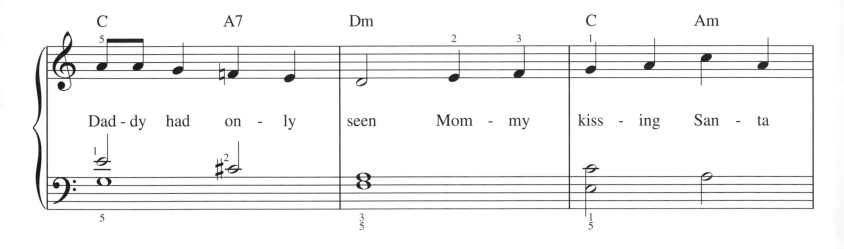

Dad - dy had on - ly seen Mom - my kiss - ing San - ta

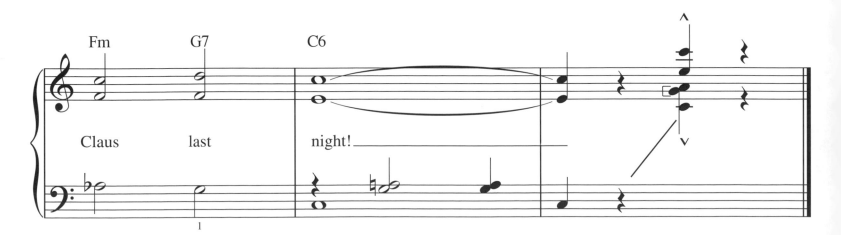

Claus last night! ____

I'LL BE HOME FOR CHRISTMAS

Words and Music by KIM GANNON
and WALTER KENT

Moderately, in 2

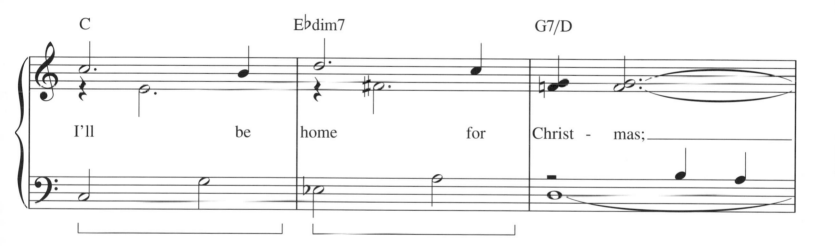

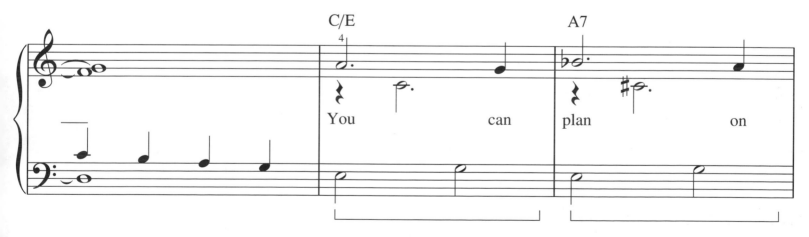

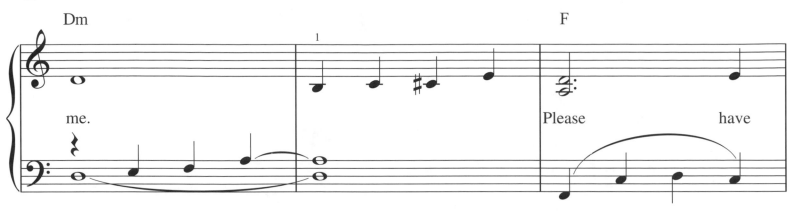

42

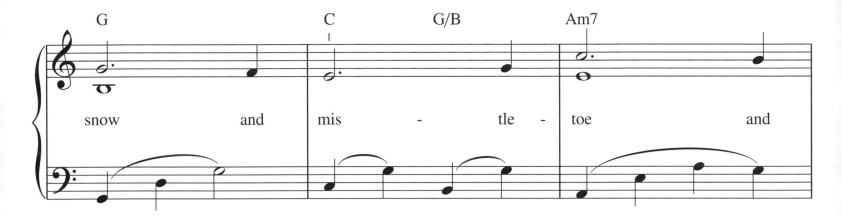

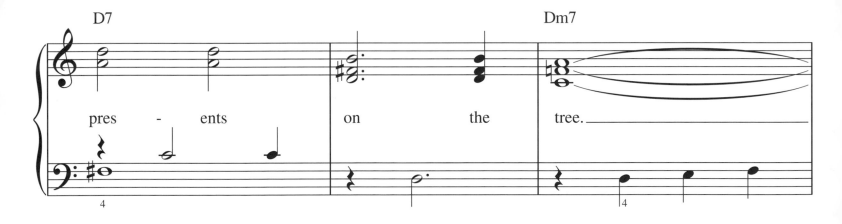

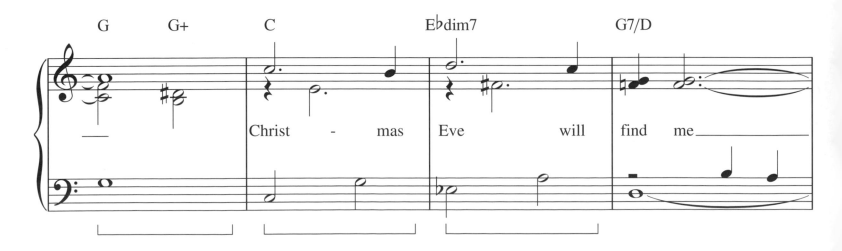

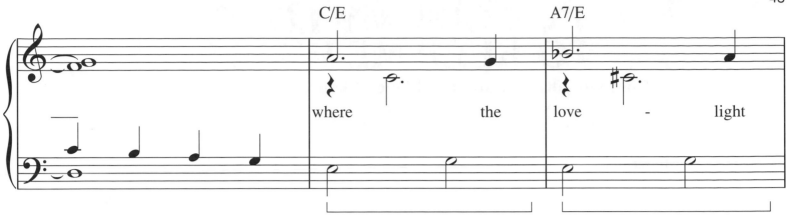

where the love - light

gleams. I'll be

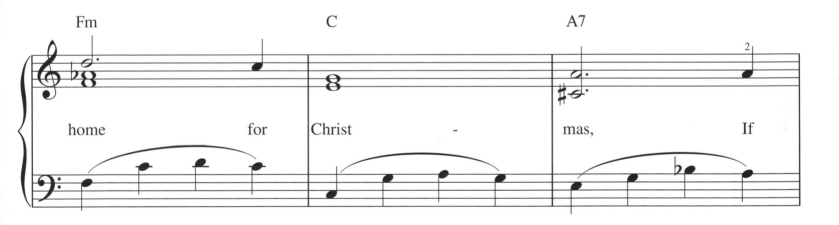

home for Christ - mas, If

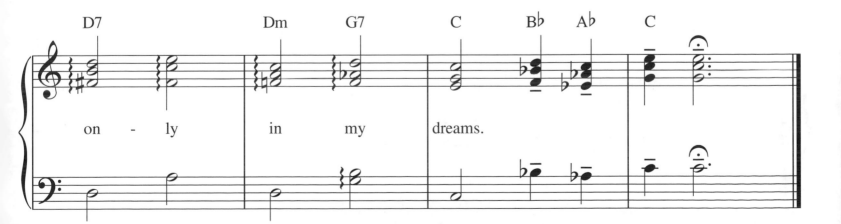

on - ly in my dreams.

I'VE GOT MY LOVE
TO KEEP ME WARM

from the 20th Century Fox Motion Picture ON THE AVENUE

Words and Music by
IRING BERLIN

Moderately

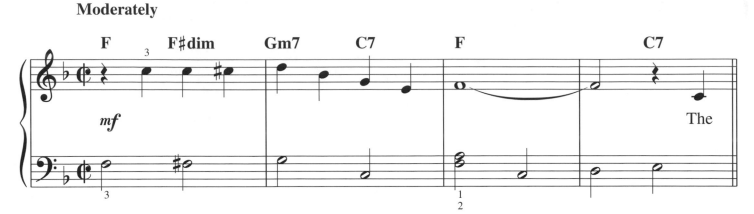

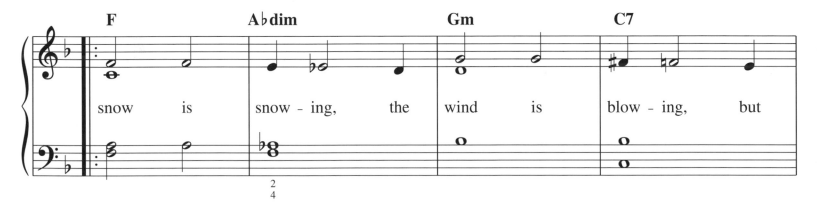

snow is snow - ing, the wind is blow - ing, but

I can weath - er the storm.

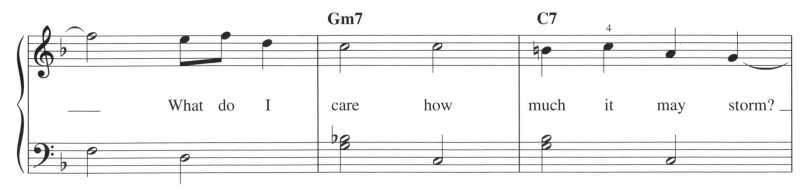

What do I care how much it may storm?

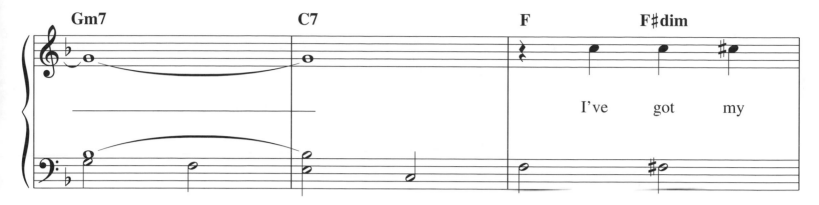

I've got my

love to keep me warm. _____ I

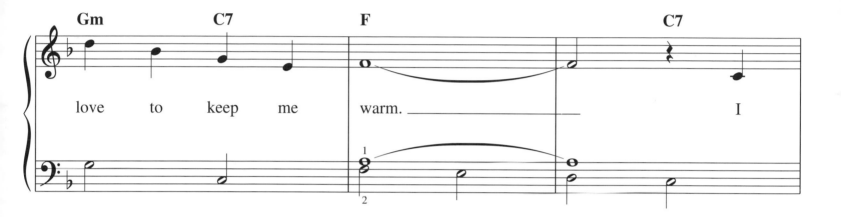

can't re - mem - ber a worse De -

cem - ber; just watch those i - ci - cles form. _____

What do I care if

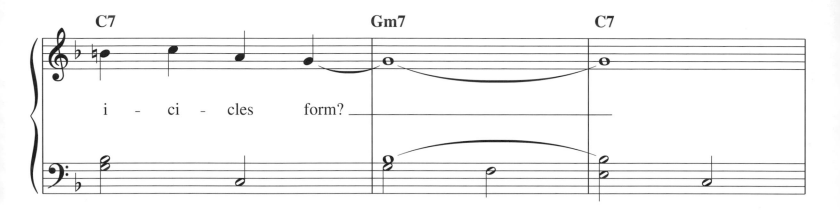

i – ci – cles form? ____

I've got my love to keep me warm. ____

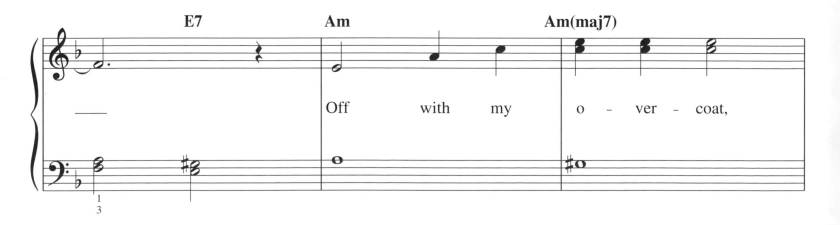

____ Off with my o – ver – coat,

off with my glove.   I need no

o - ver - coat,   I'm burn -ing with love.   My

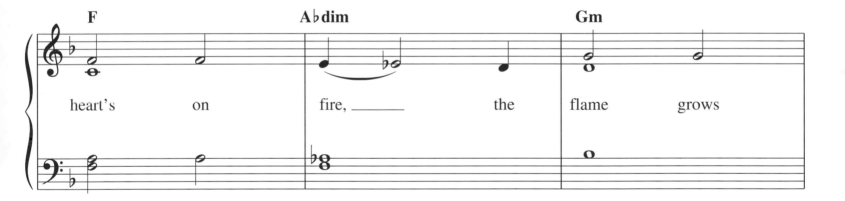

heart's on   fire, _____ the flame grows

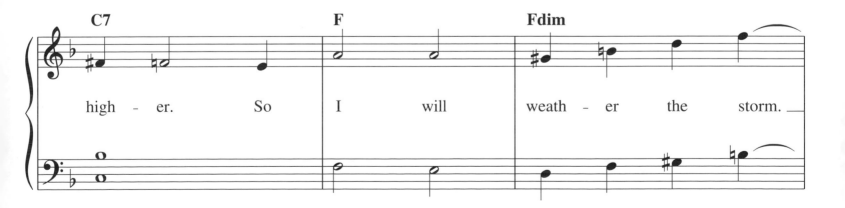

high - er. So I will weath - er the storm. __

What do I care how

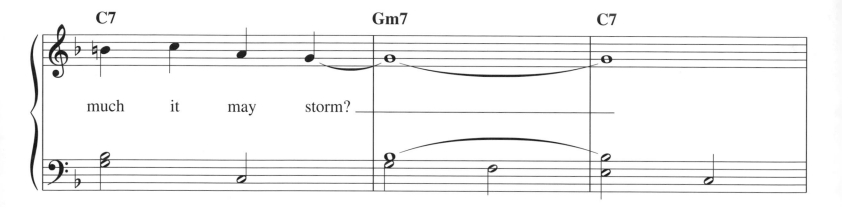

much it may storm?

I've got my love to keep me warm.

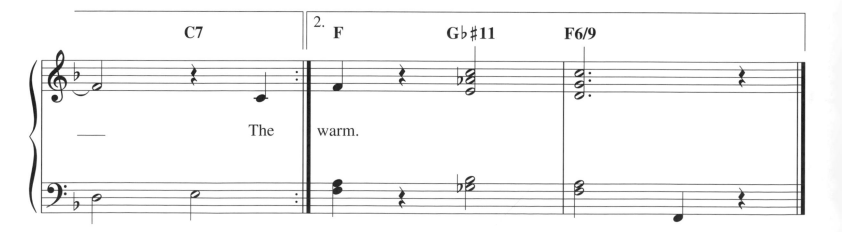

The warm.

PLEASE COME HOME FOR CHRISTMAS

Words and Music by CHARLES BROWN
and GENE REDD

Slow and bluesy

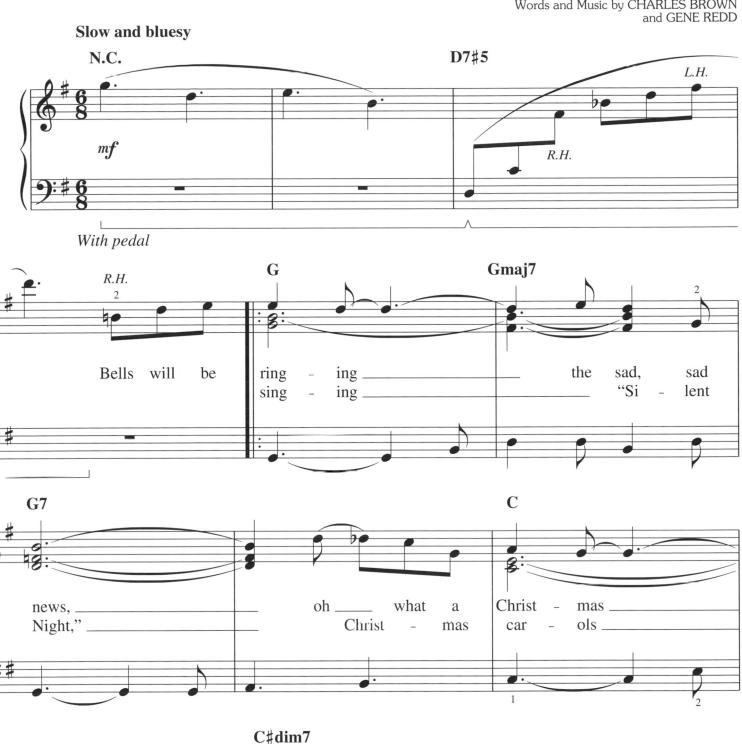

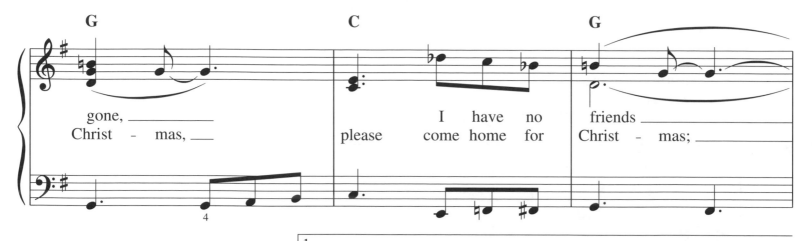

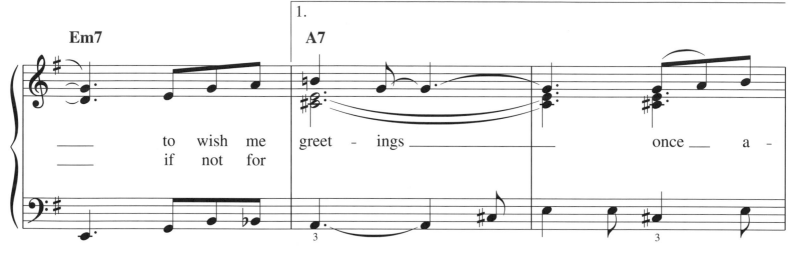

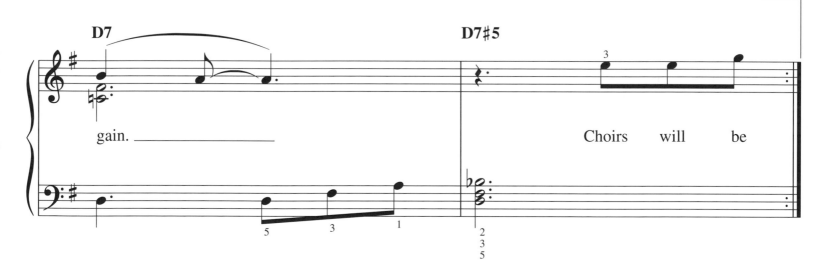

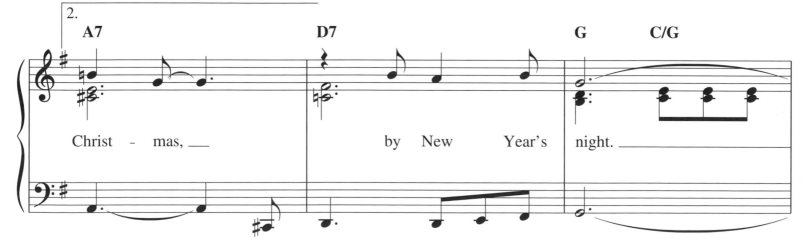

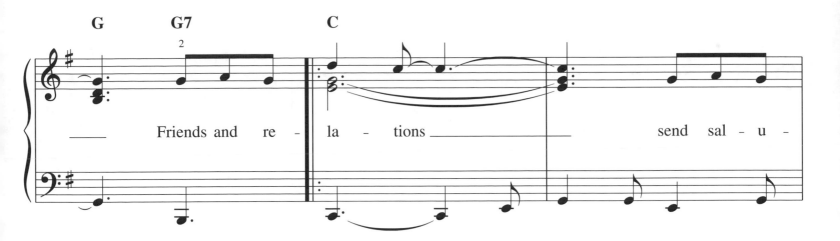

Friends and re - la - tions _____ send sal - u -

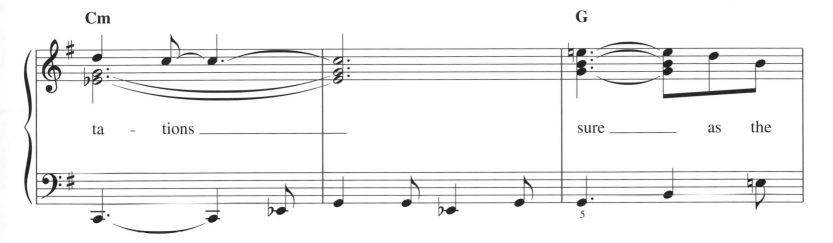

ta - tions _____ sure _____ as the

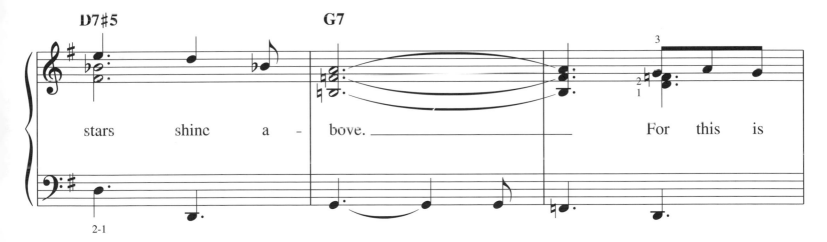

stars shine a - bove. _____ For this is

Christ - mas, _____ yes, Christ - mas my dear. _____

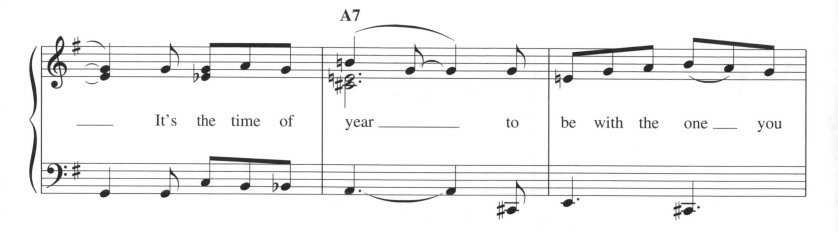

It's the time of year _____ to be with the one ___ you

love. So won't you tell me _____

___ you'll nev - er - more roam, _____ Christ - mas and

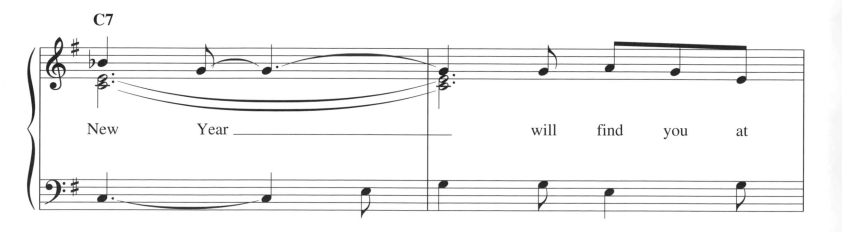

New Year _____ will find you at

C#dim7   G

home. _____   There'll be   no   more   sor - row ____

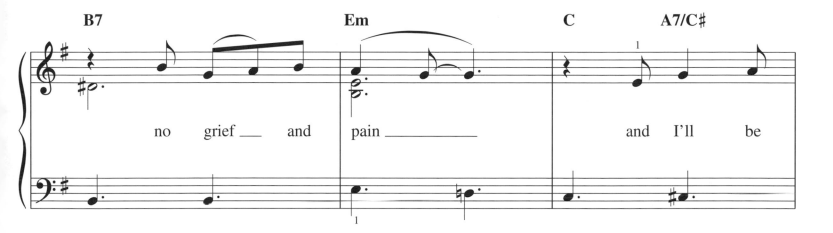

B7   Em   C   A7/C#

no   grief ___ and   pain _____   and   I'll   be

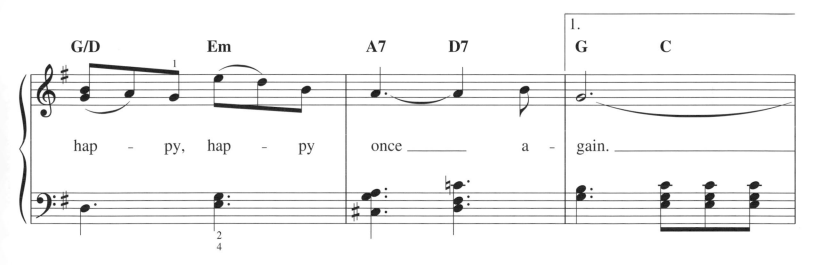

G/D   Em   A7   D7   1.   G   C

hap - py, hap - py   once _____ a - gain.

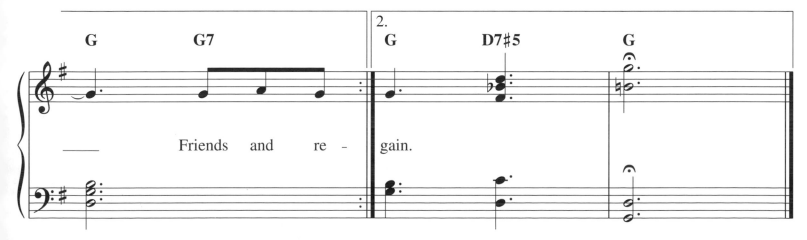

G   G7   2.   G   D7#5   G

____   Friends   and   re -   gain.

IT MUST HAVE BEEN THE MISTLETOE

(Our First Christmas)

By JUSTIN WILDE
and DOUG KONECKY

Moderately

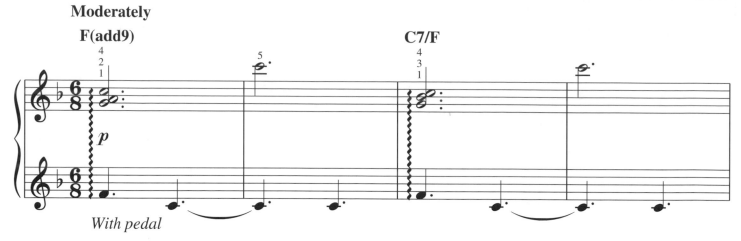

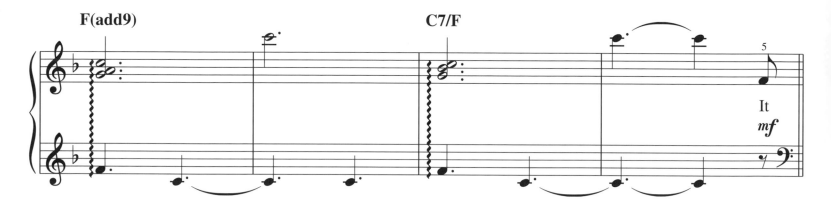

must have been ___ the mis - tle - toe, ___ the la - zy fire, ___ the

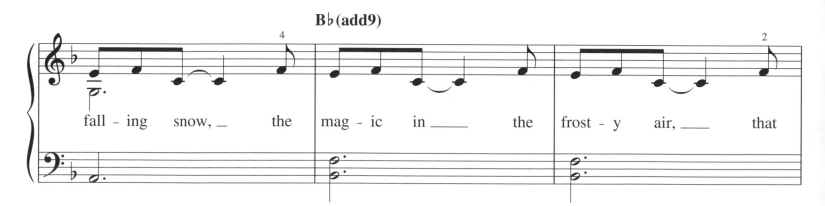

fall - ing snow, ___ the mag - ic in ___ the frost - y air, ___ that

feel - ing ev - 'ry - where. It must have been ___ the

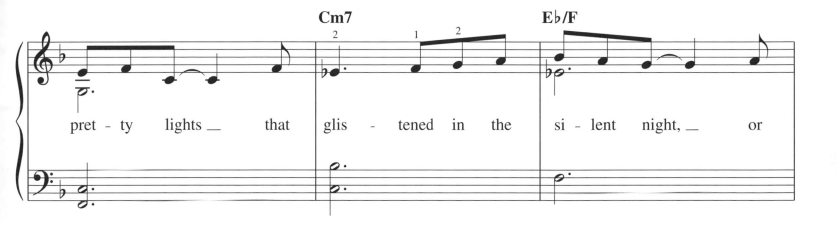

pret - ty lights ___ that glis - tened in the si - lent night, ___ or

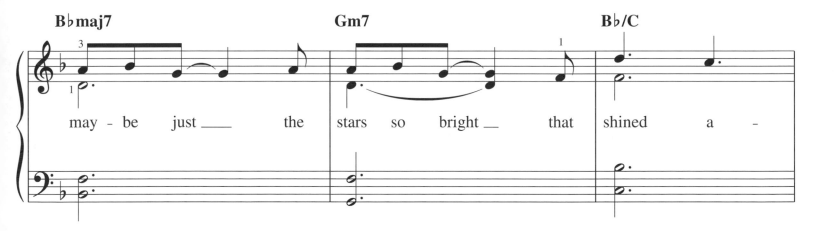

may - be just ___ the stars so bright ___ that shined a -

bove you. Our first

Christ - mas, more than we'd been

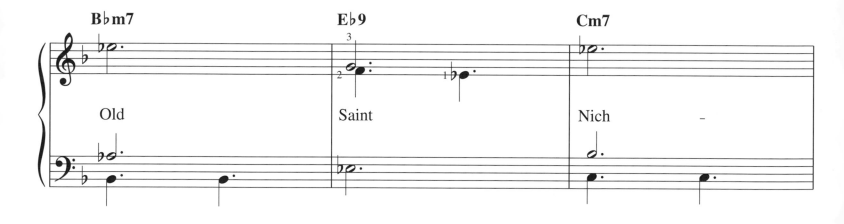

dream - ing of.

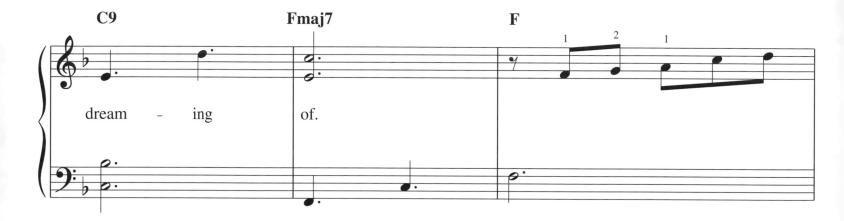

Old Saint Nich -

'las {had his fin - gers crossed that
{must have known that kiss would

we would fall in love. It could have been ___ the
lead to all of this. It must have been ___ the

hol - i - day, ___ the mid - night ride ___ up - on a sleigh, _ the
mis - tle - toe, ___ the la - zy fire, ___ the fall - ing snow, _ the

coun - try - side ___ all dressed in white, _ that cra - zy
mag - ic in ___ the frost - y air, ___ that made me

snow - ball fight. It could have been ___ the stee - ple bell ___ that
love you. On Christ - mas Eve ___ a wish come true, ___ that

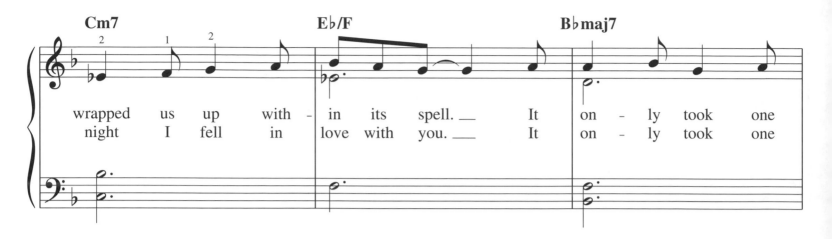

Cm7 **E♭/F** **B♭maj7**

wrapped us up with — in its spell. ___ It on - ly took one
night I fell in love with you. ___ It on - ly took one

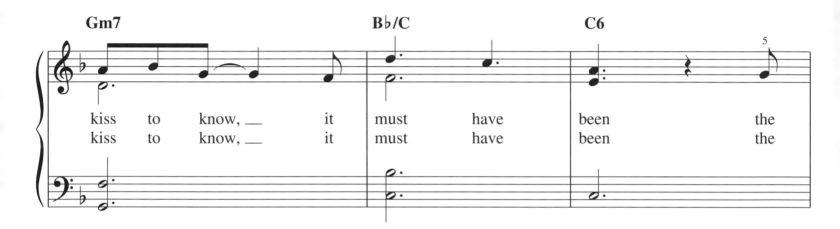

Gm7 **B♭/C** **C6**

kiss to know, ___ it must have been the
kiss to know, ___ it must have been the

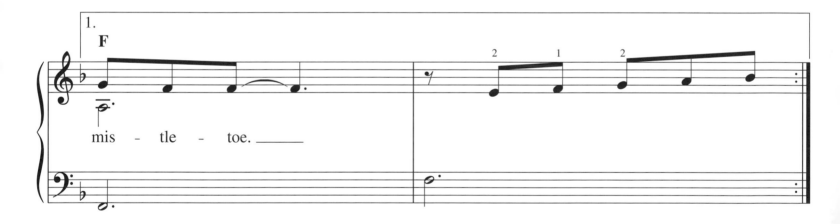

1.

F

mis - tle - toe. _____

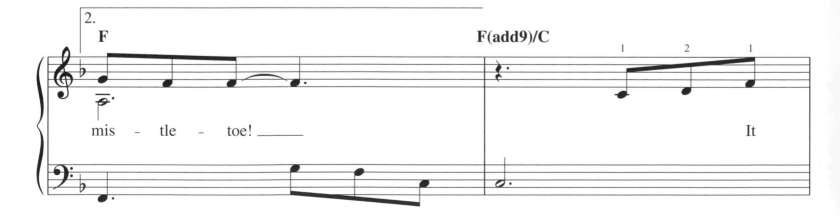

2.

F **F(add9)/C**

mis - tle - toe! _____ It

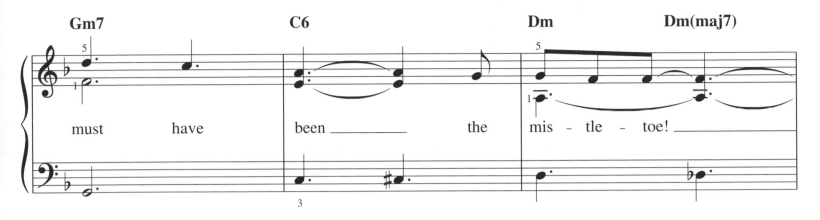

must have been _____ the mis - tle - toe! _____

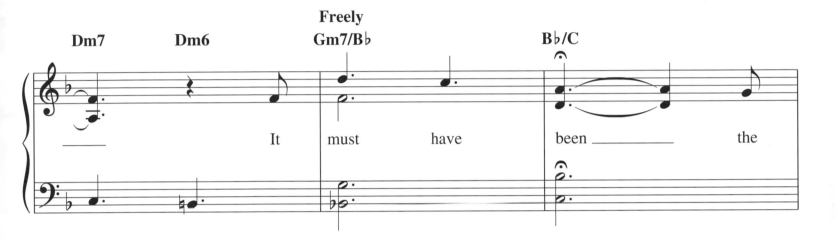

_____ It must have been _____ the

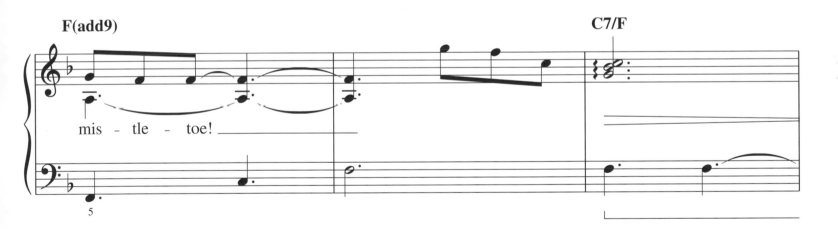

mis - tle - toe! _____

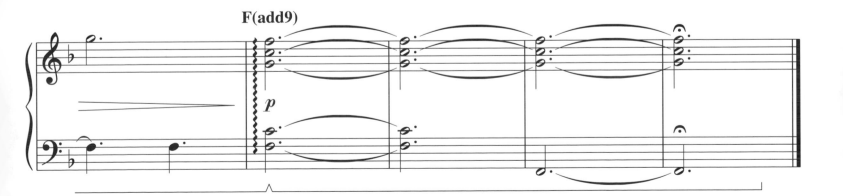

LET IT SNOW! LET IT SNOW! LET IT SNOW!

Words by SAMMY CAHN
Music by JULE STYNE

Moderately fast

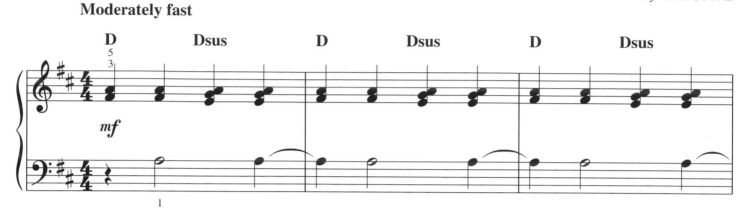

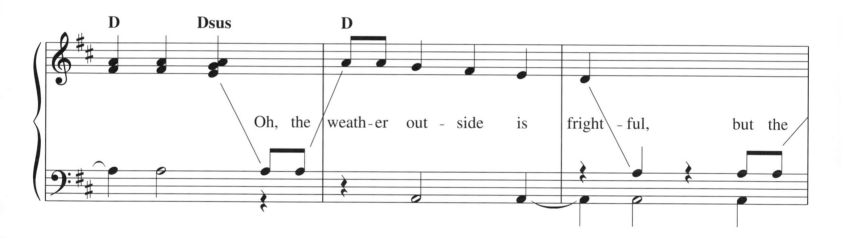

Oh, the weath-er out-side is fright-ful, but the

fire is so de-light-ful, and since we've no place to

go, let it snow, let it snow, let it snow. It

does-n't show signs of stop - ping and I

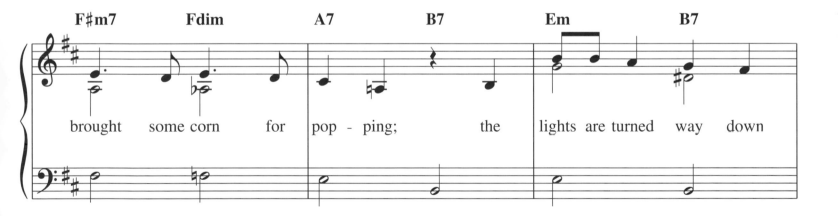

brought some corn for pop - ping; the lights are turned way down

low, let it snow, let it snow, let it snow. When we

fi - nal - ly kiss good - night, how I hate to go out in the

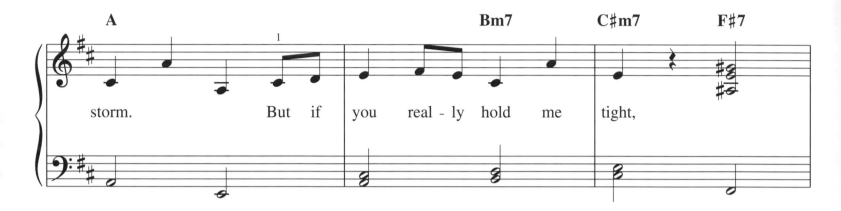

storm. But if you real - ly hold me tight,

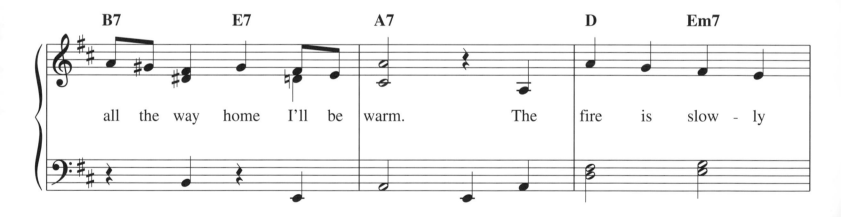

all the way home I'll be warm. The fire is slow - ly

dy - ing, and my dear, we're still good - by - ing, but as

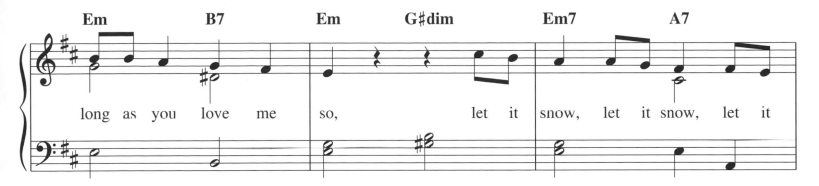

long as you love me so, let it snow, let it snow, let it

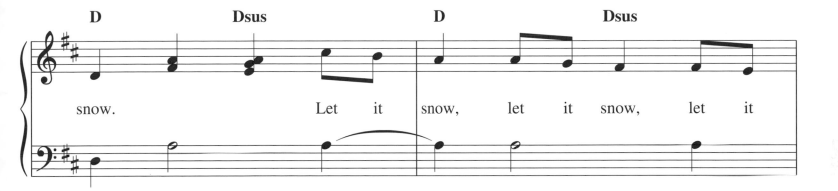

snow. Let it snow, let it snow, let it

snow. Let it snow, let it snow, let it snow. Let it

snow, let it snow, let it snow.

MERRY CHRISTMAS, DARLING

Words and Music by RICHARD CARPENTER
and FRANK POOLER

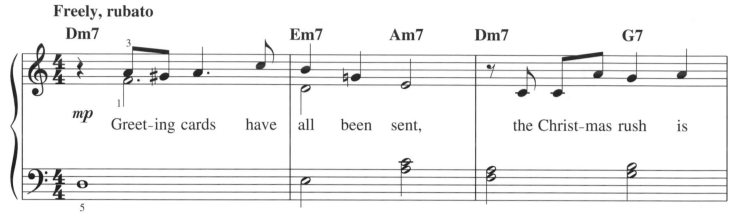

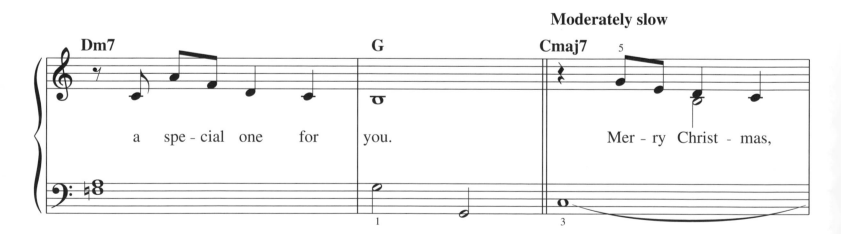

dar - ling. We'rc a - part that's true; but

I can dream and in my dreams, I'm Christ - mas - ing with

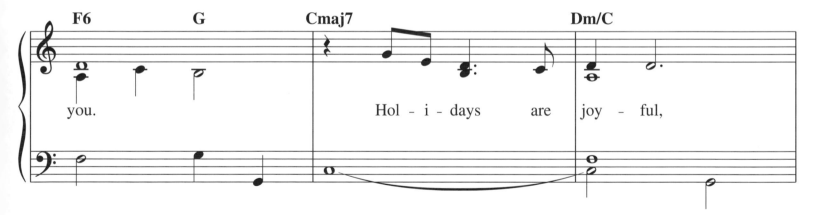

you. Hol - i - days are joy - ful,

there's al - ways some - thing new. But ev - 'ry day's a

hol - i - day   when I'm near   to   you.   The ___

lights   on my tree   I   wish   you could see,   I wish it ev - 'ry

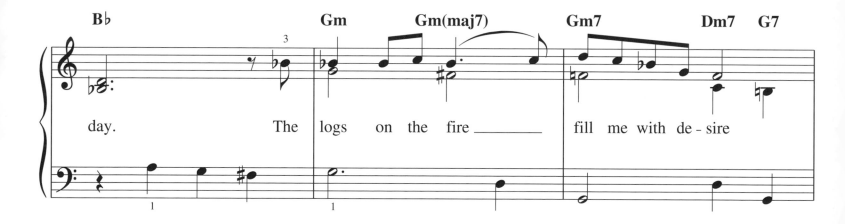

day.   The   logs   on   the   fire _____   fill   me with de - sire

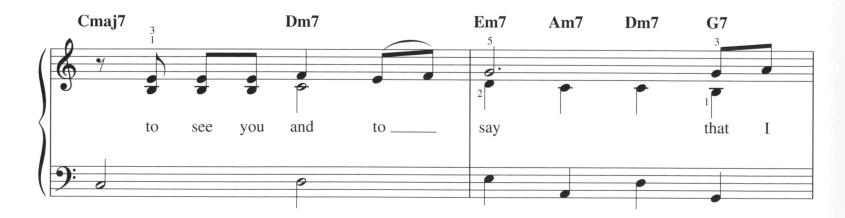

to   see   you   and   to _____   say   that   I

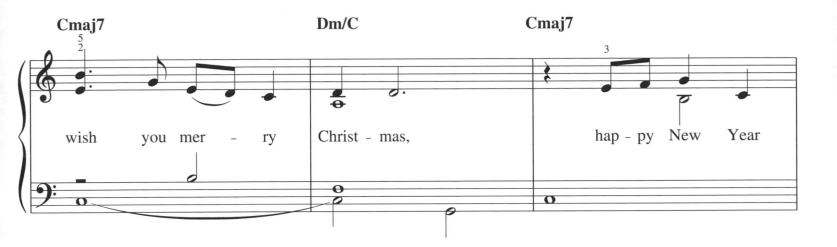

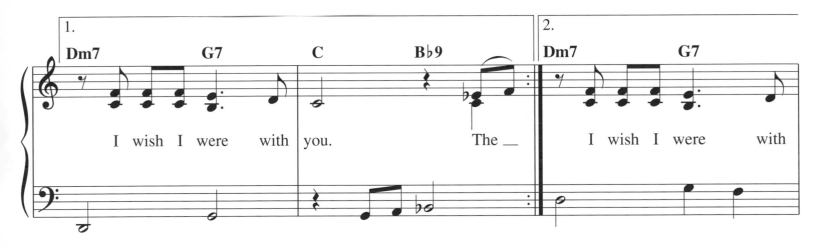

MERRY CHRISTMAS, BABY

Words and Music by LOU BAXTER
and JOHNNY MOORE

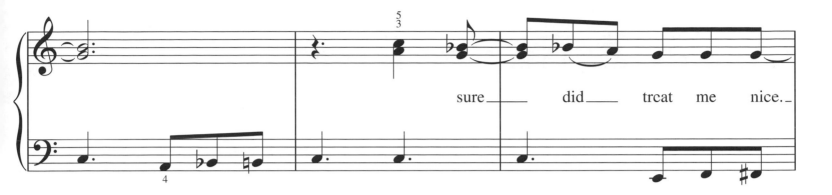

sure___ did___ treat me nice.___

Gave me a dia-

mond ring for Christ-mas, now I'm liv-ing

in par - a - dise.___

Well, I'm feel - ing might - y fine;

C7

got good mu - sic on my ra - di - o.

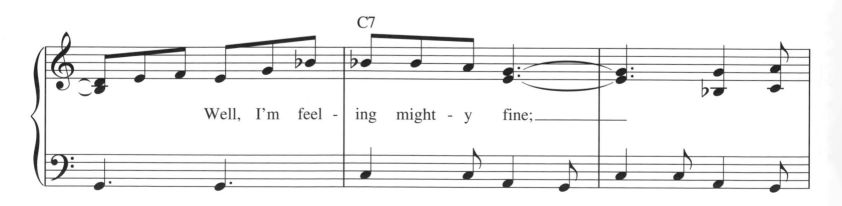

C7

Well, I'm feel - ing might - y fine;

got good mu - sic on my ra - di - o.

Well, I

wan - na kiss you, ba - by,   while you're stand - ing

'neath the mis - tle - toe.

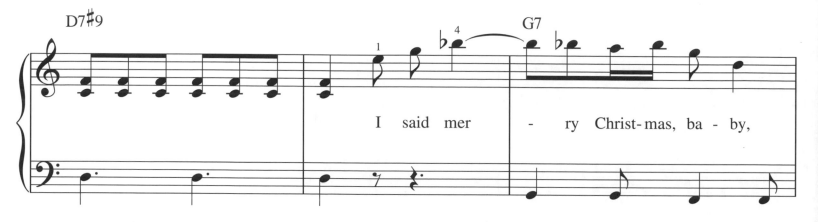

I said mer - ry Christ - mas, ba - by,

yes, you sure did treat me nice.___

___ Mer - ry,

mer - ry Christ - mas, ba - by,

well, you sure___

did___ treat me nice.

Gave me a dia-mond ring for Christ - mas,

now I'm liv-ing in___ par - a - dise.__

MERRY, MERRY CHRISTMAS, BABY

Words and Music by MARGO SYLVIA
and GILBERT LOPEZ

Slow Fifties Rock

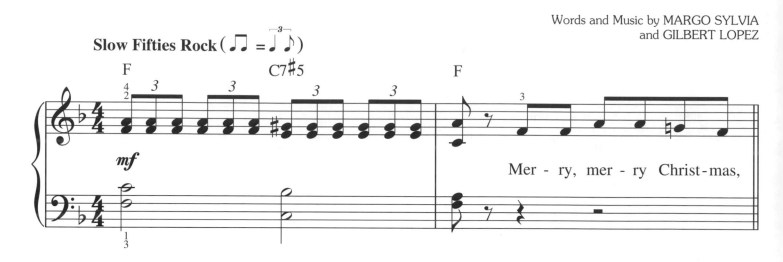

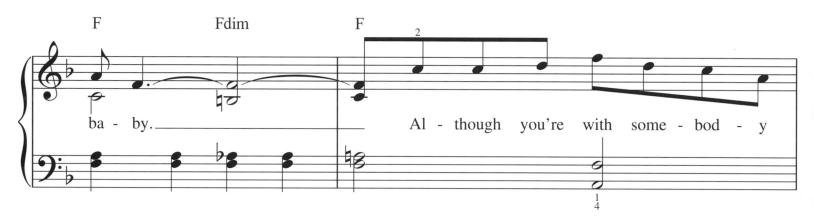

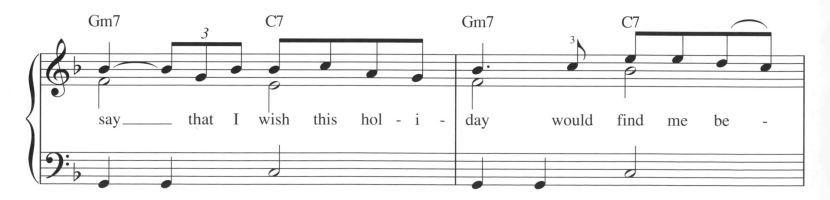

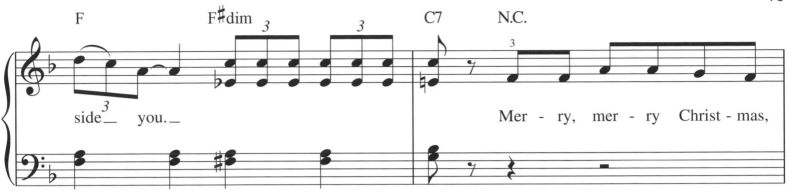

F   F#dim   C7   N.C.

side you.   Mer - ry, mer - ry Christ - mas,

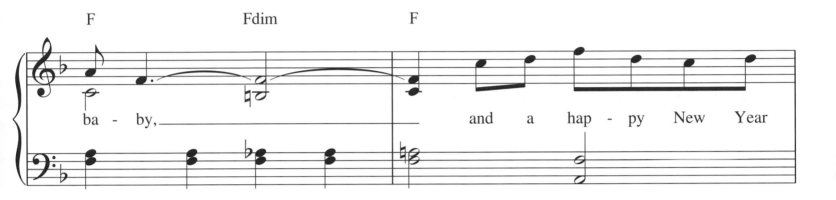

F   Fdim   F

ba - by,   and a hap - py New Year

G7   C7

too.   It was Christ - mas Eve we

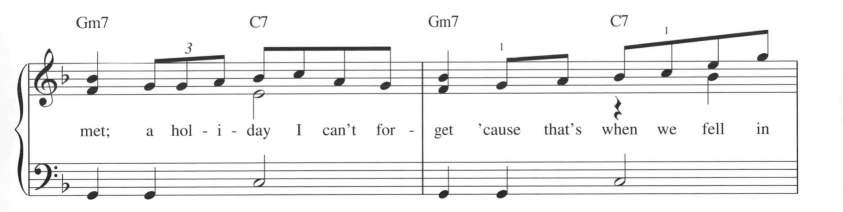

Gm7   C7   Gm7   C7

met; a hol - i - day I can't for - get 'cause that's when we fell in

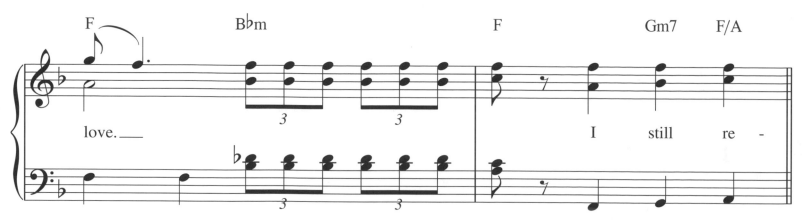

ba - by,_____ and a hap - py New Year too.__

I am hop - ing that you'll find a__ love as true as mine. Mer - ry, mer - ry Christ-mas,

ba - by. I still re - find__ a__ love as truc as

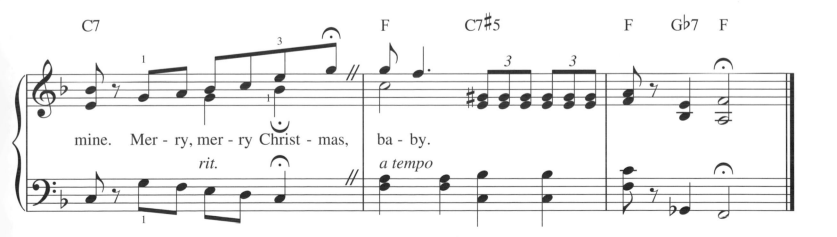

mine. Mer - ry, mer - ry Christ - mas, ba - by.

rit.   *a tempo*

MISS YOU MOST AT CHRISTMAS TIME

Words and Music by MARIAH CAREY
and WALTER AFANASIEFF

With feeling

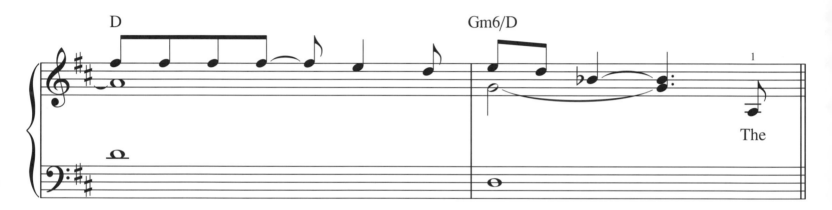

The

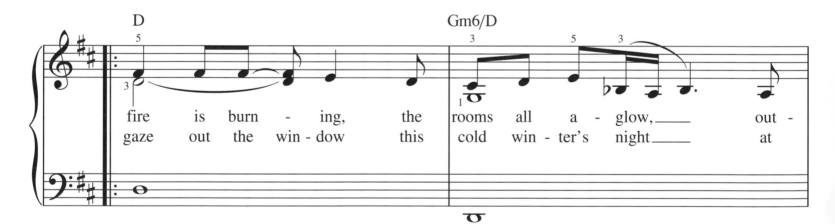

fire is burn - ing, the rooms all a - glow,___ out-
gaze out the win - dow this cold win - ter's night___ at

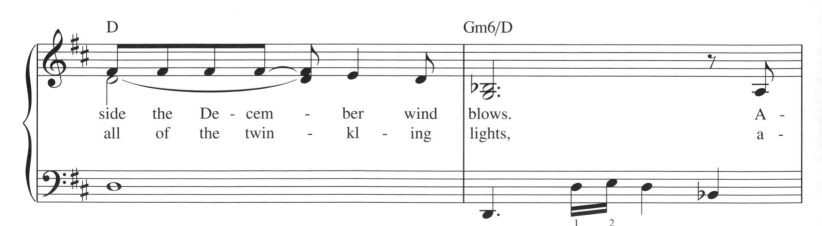

side the De - cem - ber wind blows. A -
all of the twin - kl - ing lights, a -

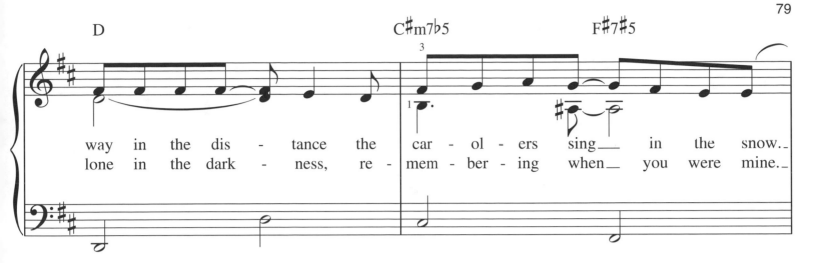

way in the dis - tance the car - ol - ers sing___ in the snow..
lone in the dark - ness, re - mem - ber - ing when___ you were mine..

Ev - 'ry - bod - y's laugh - ing, the world is cel - e - brat - ing and
Ev - 'ry - bod - y's smil - ing, the whole world is re - joic - ing and

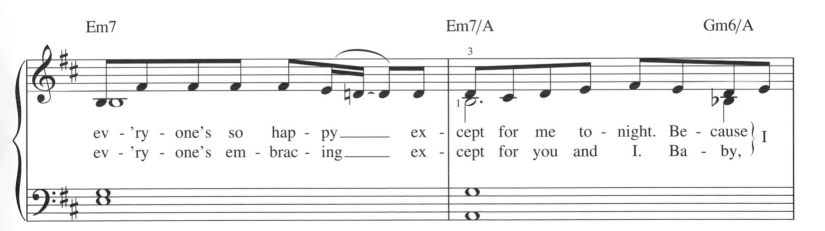

ev - 'ry - one's so hap - py___ ex - cept for me to - night. Be - cause } I
ev - 'ry - one's em - brac - ing___ ex - cept for you and I. Ba - by,

D   F#7sus   F#7

miss you_____ most at_____ Christ-mas time and I can't

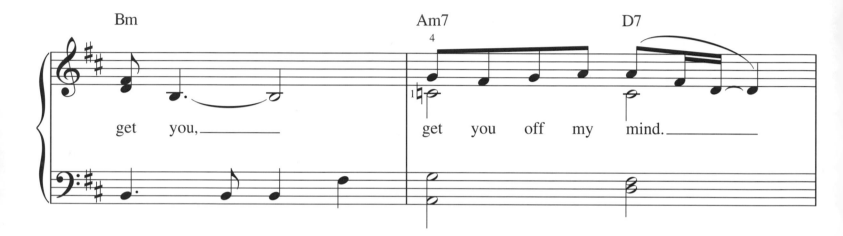

Bm   Am7   D7

get you,_____ get you off my mind._____

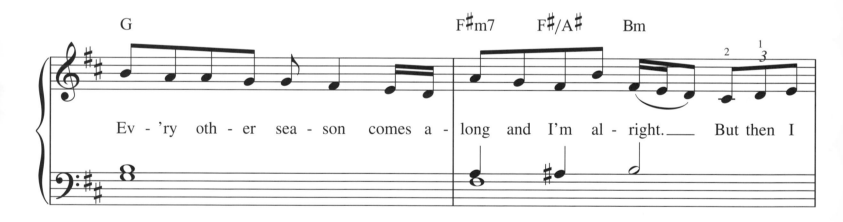

G   F#m7 F#/A# Bm

Ev - 'ry oth - er sea - son comes a - long and I'm al - right.____ But then I

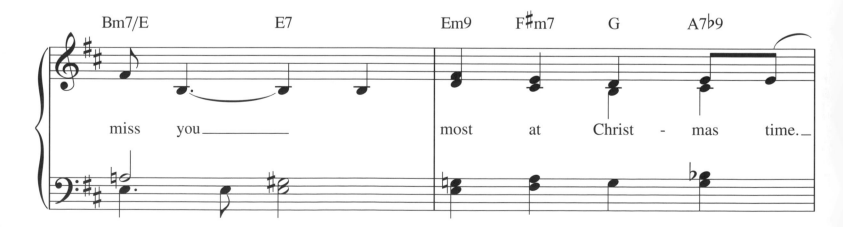

Bm7/E   E7   Em9 F#m7 G   A7b9

miss you_____ most at Christ - mas time.__

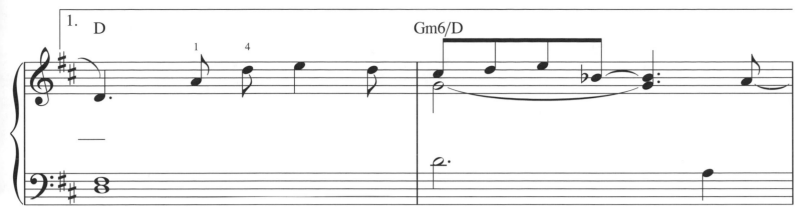

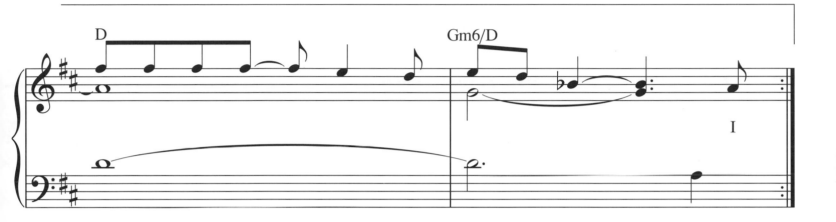

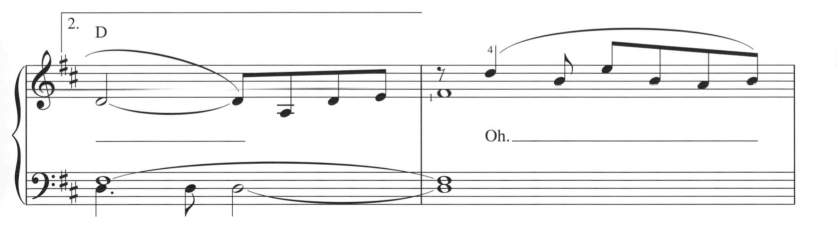

Oh._____

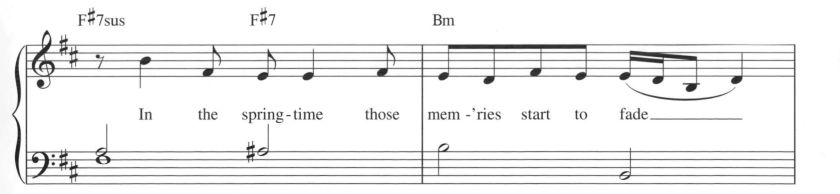

In the spring-time those mem-'ries start to fade_____

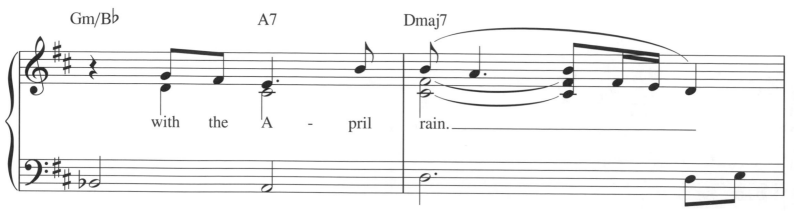

with the A - pril rain._____

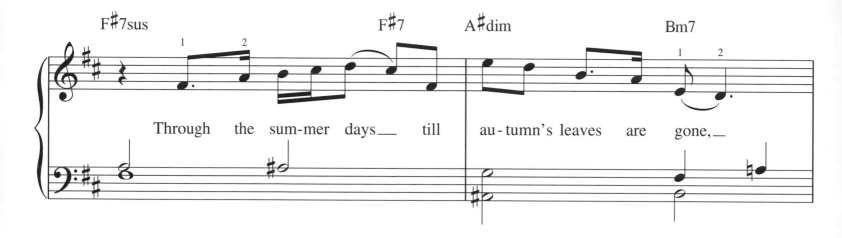

Through the sum-mer days___ till au-tumn's leaves are gone,___

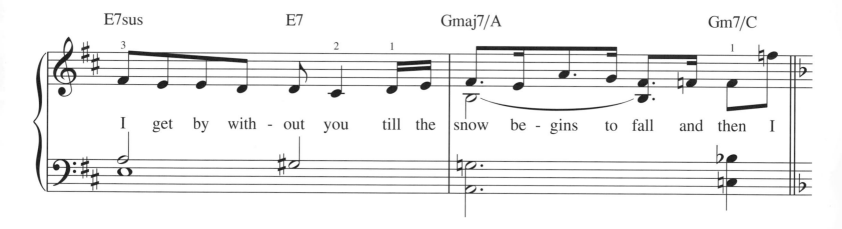

I get by with-out you till the snow be-gins to fall and then I

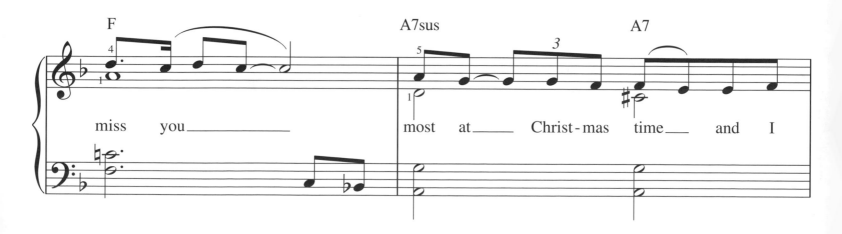

miss you_____ most at_____ Christ-mas time___ and I

can't get____ you, no - no no,____ get you off my mind.____

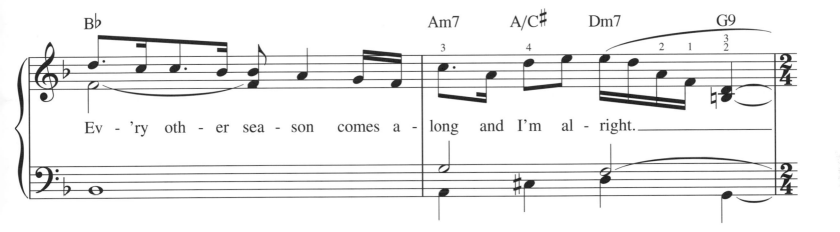

Ev - 'ry oth - er sea - son comes a - long and I'm al - right.____

But then I miss you____ most at Christ - mas

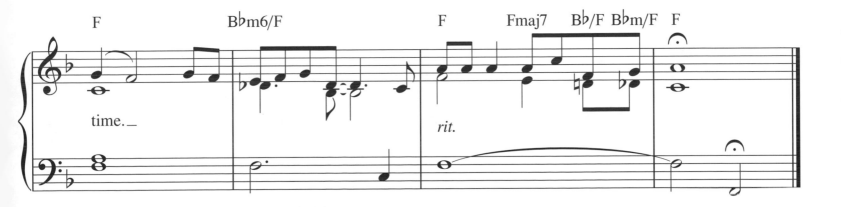

time.__ *rit.*

SANTA, BRING MY BABY BACK
(To Me)

Words and Music by CLAUDE DeMETRUIS
and AARON SCHROEDER

Bright Rock

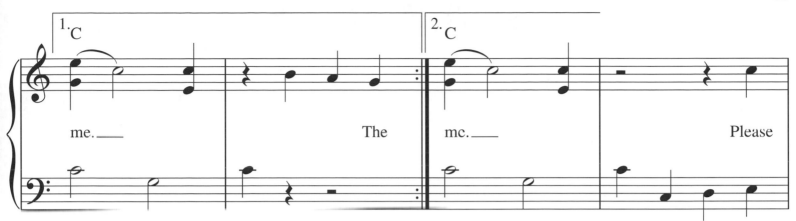

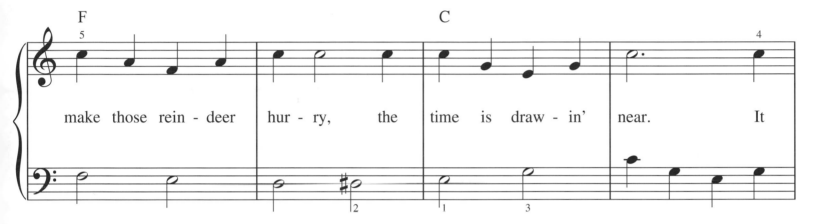

SILVER BELLS

from the Paramount Picture THE LEMON DROP KID

Words and Music by JAY LIVINGSTON
and RAY EVANS

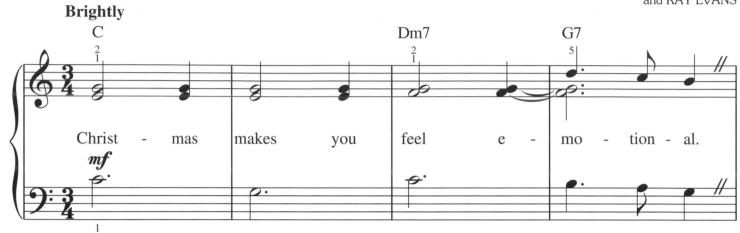

Christ - mas makes you feel e - mo - tion - al.

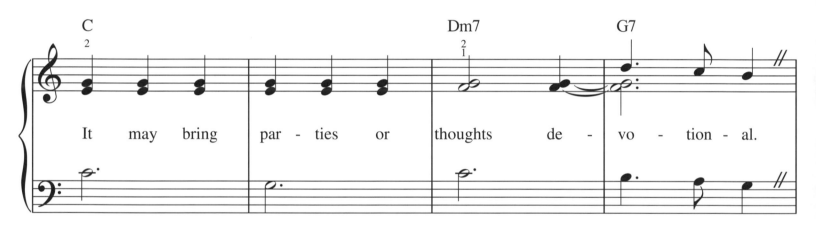

It may bring par - ties or thoughts de - vo - tion - al.

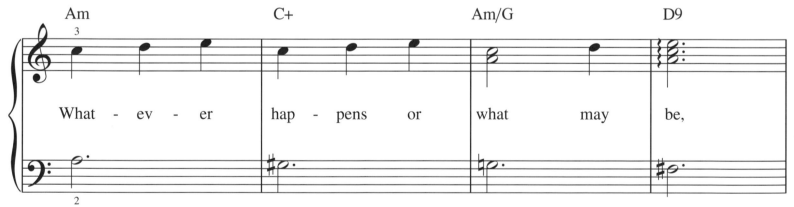

What - ev - er hap - pens or what may be,

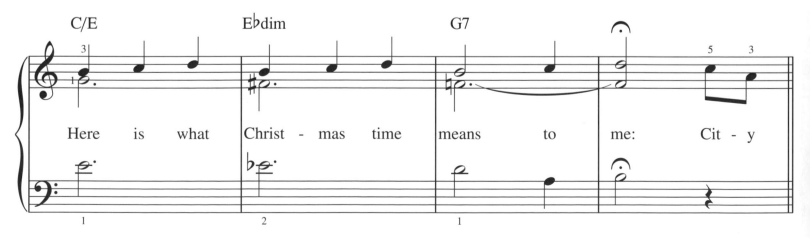

Here is what Christ - mas time means to me: Cit - y

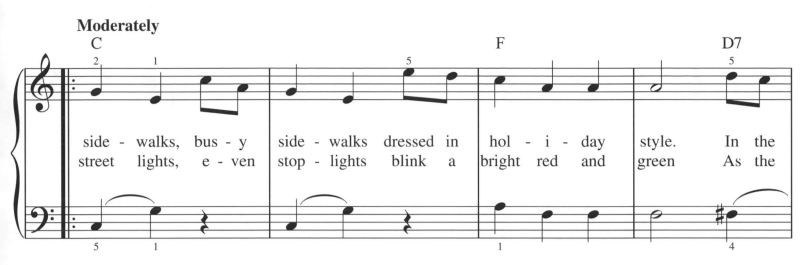

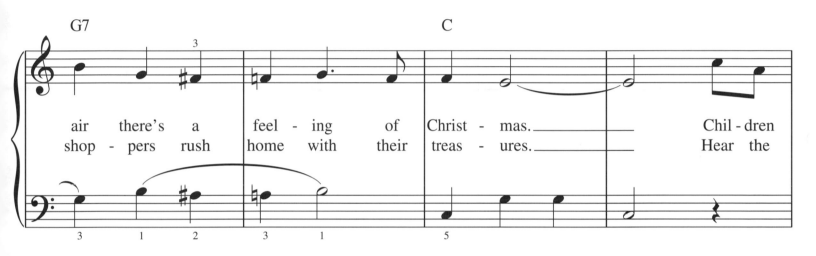

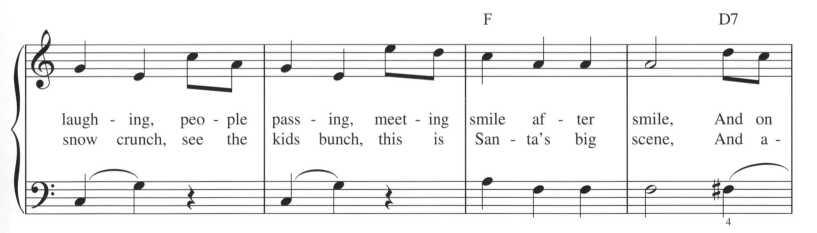

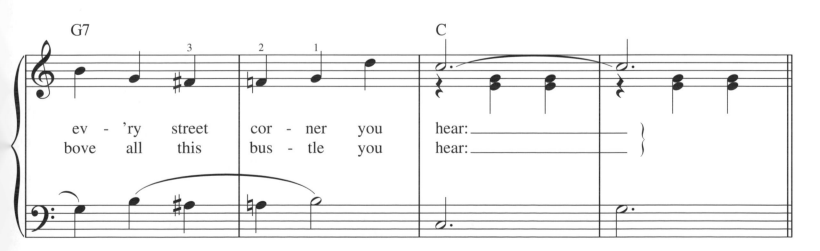

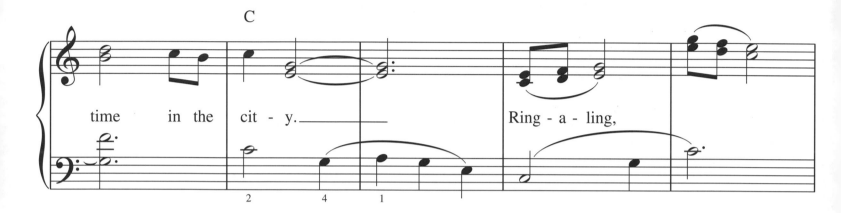

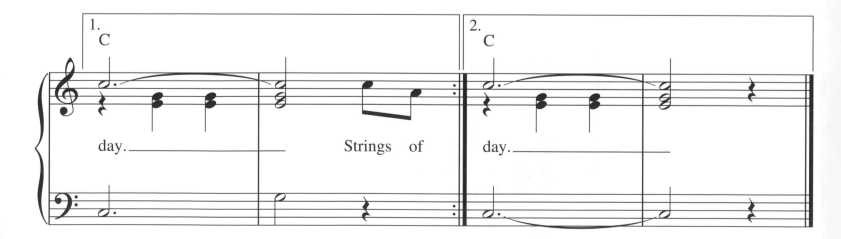